The Bishop Is Coming!

Also by Paul V. Marshall

Prayer Book Parallels:
Anglican Liturgy in America (2 vols.)

Preaching for the Church Today

The Voice of a Stranger:
On the Lay Origin of Anglican Liturgics

Same-Sex Unions:
Stories and Rites

One, Catholic, and Apostolic:
Samuel Seabury and the Early Episcopal Church

The Bishop Is Coming!

A Practical Guide
for Bishops and Congregations

PAUL V. MARSHALL

CHURCH PUBLISHING
an imprint of
Church Publishing Incorporated, New York

Cover art by Jay Sidebotham
Cover design by Corey Kent
Interior illustrations by Dorothy Thompson Perez
Interior design by John Eagleson

Church Publishing Incorporated
445 Fifth Avenue
New York, NY 10016
www.churchpublishing.org

5 4 3 2 1

Library of Congress Cataloging-in-Publication Data

Marshall, Paul Victor, 1947-
   The Bishop is coming! : a practical guide for bishops and
congregations / Paul V. Marshall.
      p. cm.
   Includes bibliographical references.
   ISBN 978-0-89869-542-7 (pbk.)
   1. Bishops. I. Title.
BV671.3.M37 2007
262'.12373 – dc22
                                                      2007003874

For Deacon George Loeffler,
On whom so much depends so often

Since the performance of a symbol is linked not to the value of its "content" as such but to its relation, one understands that it is impossible to transpose a symbolic element from one cultural or religious system into another or from one context...into another without causing it to produce effects completely different from those it had in its original system or its initial context. A gesture perfectly effective as a symbol in an African liturgy cannot, without dysfunction, be used in a Western liturgy; a posture, very meaningful in a celebration for young people, may appear inappropriate in an adult group; a sort of language or movement, well adapted to a Mass celebrated during a weekend in the woods, is apt to create a vague malaise, even with the same group of persons, if it is transported to the parish church on the next Sunday. A purely "natural" symbol does not exist.

— Louis-Marie Chauvet

Contents

Preface

This book contains far more pastoral reflection and much less specific instruction than do most how-to books. There is a reason for this. A little survey conducted in preparation for writing this book indicates the enormously high level of worry new bishops face when setting out on their journey. The number of responding bishops who hoped that their junior colleagues would be able to relax and enjoy the liturgical experience was significant enough for me to begin this discussion by acknowledging the prevalence of anxiety.

The anxiety is not evidence that everything new bishops knew about worship or the presence of God was forgotten when they were ordained to the episcopate. Responses indicate that it was precisely the seriousness with which they took their new roles that produced the anxiety, and that the anxiety was heightened because there was no accessible guide to the patterns of episcopal presidency in liturgy. Similarly, parish priests and congregations often reported frustration arising from not knowing what the bishop wanted and from concerns about timing and other mechanical problems that could be solved by joint planning. To assist all concerned in the bishop's liturgical ministry Church Publishing commissioned this little book. It focuses primarily on the visitation liturgy (with Christian initiation) and ordination. Secondary attention is given to a few other liturgical moments.

Reaffirming the Obvious

Because this book is addressed to various liturgical planners as well as to bishops, bishop-readers may occasionally have to bear with repetition of what they know well from years of ordained ministry. This is one of those moments.

Books like this one, because they present what is ostensibly clear and concrete, may create a false sense of security, a sense that the job is done when the steps are followed in order. This is the place to reaffirm what we all know: good liturgy is more than a matter of perfect performance. Consequently the reader may note that my approach to rubrics is considerably more fluid than that of other writers on ceremonial; in this regard I anticipate certain oblique descants on my song.

High, low, or avant-garde, we all seek celebrations of ritual that allow the community to deepen its experience of identity and purpose in Christ. Further, we think of a ritual practice that disperses power to God's people in word and sacrament and honors all present. It should do this without substituting good feeling for theological depth and without confusing grandiosity or sentimentality with piety. Because I have that larger liturgical goal in mind, the most I can claim for a book like this is that careful attention to the details given below can perhaps help the reader avoid some obstacles, and possibly *set the stage* for good liturgy. The reader is accordingly asked to be patient with the occasional theoretical explanation offered to illuminate the practical suggestions that are the proper scope of this book. The short bibliography offers both theoretical and practical viewpoints to some degree different from those taken here, and readers are encouraged to consult them in deciding how to proceed in their own setting. Those seeking a high level of detail are particularly referred to Howard Galley's work, *The Ceremonies of the Eucharist* (see bibliography).

In what I have just written and in pointing out that there are other thoroughly thought-out points of view available, I do not mean to minimize the importance of detail. I dare to hope that when readers have decided for themselves how to go about things, and have their own detailed plans, they will find that with the detail out of the way and technique mastered to the point where competence is unconscious, greater principles will have space to breathe life into our worship. In what follows I emphasize a certain amount of detail in the hope that when we do not have to worry *how* to do it, *what it is* will dominate our experience.

The publisher has chosen to keep this book short so that it will find a wide readership. Accordingly, it covers only the liturgies that the bishop will lead frequently, and on two occasions I have chosen not to reinvent the wheel because the descriptions of episcopal consecration and the dedication of the churches provided in Leonel Mitchell's *Pastoral and Occasional Liturgies* need no improvement.

The publisher has added a few simple illustrations so that those not experienced in vesture and ceremonial may have a better idea of what I attempt to describe.

Early on I wearied of typing "he or she" (or strained circumlocutions) when pronouns were called for, and have settled on "she" when referring to the bishop.

This is too slender and casual a volume to connect formally with the memory of that marvelous and holy polymath, Father Thomas Julian Talley, but I must acknowledge that for twenty-nine years his words and attitude have guided me in pastoral liturgy and in his beloved "liturgical science." I write with a keen sense of loss at his death early this year.

I wish to thank the bishops and priests who responded to a brief questionnaire about episcopal liturgy in ways indicating a remarkably common mind about the most pressing issues addressed here. I also am deeply grateful to the clergy and people of the Diocese of Bethlehem who continue wonderfully to bear with me as I attempt to live into the episcopate, and to Diana, who but for her limitless charity and well-known restraint could write an infinitely more entertaining account of at least one bishop in the liturgy.

+PM
Makassar Strait
Ash Wednesday, 2006

CHAPTER ONE

Bearings

"The Usual Thing"

It was 1996 and I was as new as a bishop could be. The episcopal waters were even less charted for me because I had never had the advantage of being a coadjutor or suffragan and had spent the previous eight years as a professor with only part-time duties in a very small parish. To add to the general uncertainty on this occasion, Diana and I were visiting a parish that had no rector or interim rector. Nonetheless, the liturgy got started and seemed to go well enough through sermon, confirmation, and peace. Then came the offertory. The table was set. Everything suddenly came to dead halt. Clearly something was expected from me before the offertory concluded, yet there was nothing in obvious need of blessing, elevating, or touching. People started to stare. I whispered to the deacon who always accompanies me to "find out what comes next." He inquired, and returned somewhat distraught with the message, "He says to do the usual thing."

"The usual thing" has in the following decade become code between us for situations in which we have no idea what is going to happen and no way of finding out. While we no longer worry about it very much and do go with the flow, a little sting remains, and now I cannot help but smile when I read liturgical guides that say that the liturgy "continues in the usual way."

After my jaw returned to its full upright position I simply plunged into the eucharistic dialogue, without learning what I had left out. I am comfortable enough in my role these days to just go over to somebody else and ask what is to happen, but the

1

"usual thing" experience that day in church prompted several resolutions.

The first was that I would always discuss with the rector or person in charge of each parish what happens in the key action areas that the rubrics do not explain, such as entrances, censings, offertory, the version of the Lord's Prayer to be used, and the preparation of vessels for communion.

The second was the decision to provide all parishes with an outline ("customary") of how things would flow insofar as that is my decision, leaving room for what is distinctive in the life of each parish. Priests and musicians have been very grateful to have detailed customaries, especially since those documents invite them to respond with questions or points where what I propose is not useful or not possible in their space.

We are a western church. Liturgically this has never been more true than it is in the wake of the majority of the reforms of 1979, despite the revival of a few ancient eastern texts. The original spirit of the western liturgy is simplicity and clarity, almost austerity. Recapturing this spirit was the major work of the last century's reforms in Roman, Lutheran, and Episcopal liturgy. Creative and crisp liturgy, fully expressive but without wasted time or pointless movement, happens most easily when bishops and parishes plan together and together form a sense of the arc of that day's celebration. Bishops know what they hope will happen on a given visit; the parish often has a list of things they wish to express or celebrate. These conceptions need to meet. Some bishops report meeting personally with the rector a month before the visitation to plan it in detail.

One factor that makes planning complex is the existence of those two sets of expectations. The other is that spatially no two Episcopal church buildings are the same. Thus, although it would make life simpler, one cannot provide an exhaustive point-by-point cook book with an all-inclusive recipe for every episcopal liturgy in every circumstance, as all writers concede. The specimen customaries provided at the end of this book are only that, specimens: each customary will need to be adjusted or totally replaced, depending on local circumstances. In addition to the limitations just mentioned, it is true that the prayer book provides too many textual options for one formula to fit all. Finally, the freedom enjoyed in our churches in *how* the simple ceremonial directions of the prayer book are to be carried out makes every liturgical experience something between adventure and nightmare for those who only rarely preside at liturgy in the same place two Sundays in a row. Thus a word about itinerancy seems in order.

A Wandering Minstrel, Host and Guest

None of this would matter if the bishop's appearance in a parish were simply that of a magnified supply priest or visiting dignitary. Neither is the case, however, and bishops live the identity of both host and guest at visitation liturgies. In North America we experience something historically and geographically rare in Anglicanism (and something not contemplated by other churches possessed of the episcopate, historic or otherwise). We expect that on Sundays bishops will be preaching and celebrating in the parishes in their care. It should be said in fairness that the bishops of the Roman Catholic and Orthodox Churches would be shocked to learn that there are churches such as ours which do not observe the ancient norm of the bishop presiding and preaching in the cathedral on the Lord's Day.

Rather than visiting firefighter or interesting guest speaker, the bishop comes to visit in a number of ways that have liturgical consequence.

The first is that in her own person the bishop comes as the one who has ultimate pastoral responsibility for the parish, so the weight of the event is different: the family table is fuller. Furthermore, because the bishop is by ordination and canon the chief evangelist and pastor of the diocese, the assembly rightly expects an extraordinary word of gospel proclamation and a genuine interest in its own mission. As one bishop put it, "I had to learn a new way to preach."

The second is that in these liturgies the bishop is joined at the table by the local presbyters who are the bishop's first-line colleagues. Certainly every liturgy on every occasion should look and feel like a team effort of the entire assembly. But when the bishop and colleagues stand together at the table it is to demonstrate that clergy are also part of a team of colleagues — there are to be no Lone Rangers or Wonder Women hiding inside collars. The visitation is a good time to enact ritually the truth that presbyters are not ordained because the bishop cannot be everywhere: presbyters are ordained so that the bishop's ministry can indeed be everywhere. According to the formularies of this Church, presbyters and bishops form one thing, a college in which no member acts independently or arbitrarily. The more we enact this truth liturgically the more we may come to inhabit it effectually. When liturgists speak of a norm, they do not refer to what necessarily happens as a rite is routinely celebrated, but to the characteristics of the rite in its fullness. The norm, the fullest expression, of the eucharist is the gathering of all the people together with their bishop, priests, and deacons as a community of the altar. This is the original meaning of the *circumadstantes* in the old Roman canon, all those "standing around" the holy table.

The third factor is that very often the presence of the bishop means that seldom-seen liturgical rites (confirmation, blessings of chrism, church buildings and equipment) are celebrated. Questions will arise about how much of these rites require explanation, and how and when that explanation is given. Some dioceses provide bulletin inserts explaining the occasion; others rely on rectors to prepare the parish for what it will experience. All should relax with the idea that no one will be out of the building in an hour, just as we know that Thanksgiving dinner lasts longer than the usual family meal.

The fourth is that the presence of the bishop is meant to connect the parish with the larger community of which it is a part, so the liturgy ought to feel a little different. The parish ought to become aware that its table is part of a larger board. This task is becoming more difficult because increasing numbers of laity and clergy in the church are from non-episcopal or non-liturgical traditions and really have very little grasp of our ecclesiology. This connection is not necessarily made by liturgical grandeur or reproducing cathedral liturgy in a wayside chapel: *Aida* performed in a shoebox can never edify, and such events ought not be attempted. However, the slight alterations in text (for example, the episcopal blessing), the number of people involved, the overall thickening of context, and in most cases the increase in vesture and insignia, create the sense of contact with what is not normally quite so much a part of consciousness: each parish is, as Bishop Claude Payne brilliantly said, a missionary outpost of the diocesan effort to follow Jesus and make him known. Beyond this, if the postmodern movement succeeds in its announced agenda of increasing our sensitivity to mystery, all these shifts in context and content should enhance the ability of the episcopal visitation to help the parish feel more deeply its connection to the matrix in which its ministry is situated.

Finally, since it is a special occasion and involves the chief pastor, there will be anxiety, despite the bishop's attempt to put everyone at ease. Some of that anxiety is part of the fun: people are doing something special and would like what they have planned to come off well; they want to look their best — in every culture it is what people do when company comes. The poor of the developing nations have a great deal to teach most of us about celebration in this very respect. I have deliberately used the word fun. Until the joy of knowing and praising God in the community of the redeemed is a species of fun, liturgy will fall flat.[1]

---

1. It is said that long ago, while Russia was still in the hands of the communists, a very serious and devout lady of the Church of England observed a Russian monk in then-Leningrad, admiring his devotion under persecution. Not being of a very high church background herself, her experience of Russia was leading her to wonder about the possibilities of ritual to sustain persecuted people, although she would not have put it that way. She finally summoned the courage to ask him, reverently, "Father, why do you and your people kiss the icons?" The monk

There is a freeing word in all of this: given all the variety of place and circumstance that faces the visiting bishop, the bishop can be assured that almost no liturgy will go exactly right — these are live performances as compared with studio recordings, where every track can be endlessly revised until a perfect sound is produced. While we care and we try, the goal is to get from the beginning to the end in a way that enacts the drama, assuming all the while the imperfection of our service. Public displays of irritation over mistakes made by liturgical assistants have in fact had far-reaching consequences; unkind words uttered during the liturgy have been known to propel people out of what fragile relationship with God they had been able to maintain. Custody of the eyes includes not rolling them.

We cannot resolve here the enormous tension between catholic ideal and congregationalist reality that complicates pastoral and liturgical life in the Episcopal Church. Those tensions play themselves out differently according to the diocese, bishop, rector, and parish involved in a given visitation. We can try to respond to what each place could reasonably expect of its bishop and to honor the integrity of their community. The more challenging part is to do that while not *becoming* someone other than one's self, maintaining integrity and self-definition while respecting theirs.

Seldom does this mean conscientiously doing something unfamiliar to a parish or declining to do something people are used to. More commonly it means trying to maintain a persona that is genuinely and recognizably oneself no matter the circumstances, the episcopal version of the Stoic ideal. This is as important in preaching as it is in presiding: if the presence and voice in the pulpit are significantly different from the presence and voice in the sacristy or parish hall, nobody is fooled or helped. True transparency in preaching and prayer comes from lack of affectation. This applies doubly in the liturgy, where the affected voice or unnatural gesture can betray the cleavage in the presider's own

---

drew himself up to all five feet of his stature, paused, stroked his beard, and said, "Bee-cohse . . . it's fun."

soul and disorient the worshiper. If necessary, it is well to pretend to be unaffected and grow into it! Youth are not beguiled by old people trying to speak more than a word or two of their language. They develop their language primarily to separate themselves from their elders.

In the film noir *Dead Again,* defrocked psychiatrist Robin Williams gives advice to gumshoe Kenneth Brannagh, who is trying to quit smoking but seemingly cannot. Williams tells him that ultimately there are smokers and non-smokers, concluding, "Find out what you are and be that." There are bishops whose style and presence I admire profoundly, but for a host of reasons cannot emulate, and I must live with that. I can never be mesmerizing or very extroverted, but I can be unaffectedly my best self. Liturgy works when the presider addresses God and the assembly from the core of the relationship she actually has with each.

It follows then that the maintenance of our own spiritual life will shape our style of liturgical presidency. As our lives enter ever further into the mystery, our leadership of worship may evolve towards a rich simplicity. In the movie just mentioned, I think Williams' line is meant to propel Brannagh's character into choosing who he will be, an essentially spiritual decision. Surely they who wish to lead liturgy effectively will be propelled into a place where their own spirituality deepens. Far too much in the episcopate can drive us away from our spiritual foundations, with personally and liturgically harmful effect. The last thing one wants to be is a technician of the sacred, personally alienated from that which is celebrated. The one genuinely poignant moment in the somewhat busy pilot episode of TV's "The Book of Daniel" occurred when Daniel asks Jesus, seated beside him in his Volvo wagon, if the Lord also speaks to his father, the bishop. There is a beat and Jesus wistfully says, "I used to."

I was traveling with an Englishman who said of someone on our ship, "He combines the arrogance of a surgeon and the vanity of a bishop." He was unaware of my profession, so the words had special impact. Not all surgeons are arrogant and not all bishops are vain, but each profession certainly offers manifold temptation along those lines. I leave the medical profession to tend its own issues but can assert that the deference paid to bishops along with certain aspects of our liturgical life can tempt one to a pernicious species of vanity. Daily self-examination is necessary in this regard. A serious impediment to effective liturgical leadership is, as innumerable ordination sermons mention, letting the mitre go to one's head. I have found repeated reading of Thomas Cahill's *Pope John XXIII* (New York: Penguin, 2002) a great help fighting this battle, both for the good example it celebrates and the many horrific tales it tells from church history.

Given that what follows in this book resembles something between a recipe collection and a football playbook, the reader may indulge my recalling that our effective liturgical presence will never exceed our own spirituality as it is disciplined by preparation and communal planning. *The spirituality of a group cannot exceed that of its leader.* If the leader puts on the persona of a game show host, the assembly will degenerate into an audience. Put another way, the fundamental itinerancy of our bishops and the relative fluidity of parish liturgical practices necessitate the bishop's having a clear sense of self and leading worship from that clearly defined self. It also necessitates everyone's being in on the plan and allowing themselves to be who they are and can be in Christ.

Liberating Constraints

A bishop told me regarding this project, "I wish somebody had told me that it is more important to lead the worship of the people of God than it is to do things right." I found that statement profoundly true on one hand and a bit curious on the other. I agree that the focus of liturgical ministry must be on worship of the Father in the name of Jesus and the power of the Spirit. My colleague is certainly right to point out that when one lets go of performance anxiety or worse, any fixation on doing things right for obsessive-compulsive reasons, the liturgical event can come alive. At the same time, leading worship is itself a liturgy — a word that actually means work done for the sake of others. What is done for others requires skill, love, and effort. Six parts sincerity to one part "it's how I felt" is an entirely appropriate attitude for any activity of life — when there is nobody else in the room. When any activity is public there are some liberating constraints that I would like to observe.

The first constraint: everyone shall have due respect and consideration. Our grandparents understood this as the essence of all etiquette. Whether we are considering a homecoming dance, a first date, a meeting, dinner with friends, a football game, or attendance at a concert, activities that involve more than one person have to be constructed so that all present are appropriately recognized, and everybody gets more or less what they are entitled to. When those equities are not observed, it is usually at someone's expense. The more crowded the event, the more organized its procedures must be to be sure that everyone is given their due and no one is imposed upon or taken for granted. When the bishop is present as chief pastor of the community, it is vitally important that all present receive their due, and that the bishop practice the discipline of keeping the focus on the assembly.

The second constraint: whether our stance is evangelical or catholic we cannot disregard the fact that organized worship is a complex of rituals. Rituals are actions that carry and express values. Rituals create and strengthen identity and purpose; at root they connect people. The most complicated ritual in America today is the "wave" at a football stadium, where tens of thousands of people perform a coordinated act symbolizing their identity as The Crowd and their joy at being together at the event. Family meals and love-making are examples of highly ritualized activities where variety occurs within a framework of agreed upon behaviors, even between people newly married. Disregarding the ritual nature of any event inevitably brings too much attention to the protagonist or host and moves the nature of the event away from a coordinated effort in which all know their parts and toward a show with a star and supporting cast. Low or high in ornamentation and choreography, public worship needs to be planned and led with care, so that innate human capacity for ritual can do its connecting job.

That observation leads to *the third constraint: good ritual disperses power rather than collecting it in the person of the president*. A sermon-less, non-communicating high mass (now a thing of the past) is an example of the worst kind of bad ritual under this rubric, because all power flowed toward the altar and those who officiated at it. Similarly, not discounting the inspiration they undoubtedly bring to many, the productions of many television ministries have only one star and the members of the assembly are always pictured with expressions of adoration. Traditional liturgy intends something else, hence its relative unpopularity in the entertainment culture. That something else is about dispersing power. For example, in a case that usually does not involve bishops, we gather all the forces of church and community at the blessing of a marriage in order to empower the new couple, who are then returned to society in order to serve it. Even ordinations, which can look rather regal when done badly, have the same rhythm: the gathered church (ideally the diocese) brings forth individuals and prays mightily over them, adding vesture and other marks of office and function — and immediately receives them back as servants and leaders.

Given the constraint of power flow, one has to be ruthless about discovering how one presides. It is useful to get a friend unobtrusively to videotape a few celebrations and then to look hard: which way did the power ultimately flow in this rite? If the net effect is how grand or simple it all was, or how heroic or charming the leader or preacher was, power has been stolen or at least diverted. Readers unfamiliar with evaluating liturgy might profit from Bernadette Gasslein's work, listed in the Bibliography.

The fourth constraint follows from the previous observation: the bishop is both host and guest in the liturgy at visitations. The bishop presides, preaches a gospel word, and administers sacraments, and thus in many ways acts the host. At the same time, this parish is not the place where the bishop usually dwells, and people extend hospitality in many ways that need acknowledgment. This state of things is not apparent to many lay people. Thus bishops get used to the enthusiastic (or sometimes slightly hostile) person saying, "Welcome to our church, Bishop." There is no point in deflecting such a greeting by countering with "it is my church too," because greetings are not debates and the truth will ultimately have to be experienced by the congregation. I mention it to steel the new bishop for the shock, and because in the slightly unsettling business of itinerancy, there is also an experience of dispossession that helps one identify with Jesus, having no sacristy in which to lay one's head and no regular pulpit in which to develop a theme over several weeks. One does the best one can and moves on. It is frustrating, humbling, and yet freeing to be a bishop on the road. The parable of the sower came to mean a great deal to me after only a short time in episcopal ministry.

The more thoroughly one knows the part, the freer one is to be genuinely present and spontaneous in it.

CHAPTER TWO

Brief Survival Guides

Emergency minimal survival: wear the mitre on the way in until you reach the altar, and again from the blessing until reaching the door; carry the staff in the left hand while wearing the mitre.

Evangelical alternatives to the mildly catholic stance taken at some points in this book is the work of Colin Buchanan cited in the Bibliography. However, with the exception of the ordination rites I believe that the present work describes the statistical norm of liturgical practice in the church.

1. A Basic Guide for Bishops

This section assumes a Sunday eucharist at which confirmation, reception, and reaffirmation are celebrated. Baptism is included in the longer treatment of visitation liturgy in Chapter Three, where much of what follows will be treated in detail. I have italicized thoughts that might be new or not generally accepted information in the Episcopal Church, and those points will receive special discussion below.

I have attempted here to adapt late twentieth-century re-formed western consensus to the life and traditions of our church. That consensus, although genuinely ecumenical, has been largely guided by the Roman Catholics, because they have what sports fans would call the biggest bench to deploy in this study, but I hope that the distinctive Anglican perspective will be clear at all necessary points. While the growing consensus of liturgical and near-liturgical churches is impressive, at some points distinctive insights deserve preservation, especially where matters of ecclesiology are involved.

Before all, the bishop should have a copy of the complete liturgy for the day, along with local variations clearly spelled out, two or three weeks before the event. This enables the bishop to prepare and if necessary, to discuss questions with liturgical planners. If the parish is printing out the complete service, it is essential that the bishop check it carefully before letting it go to press.

Liturgical and musical texts should also be provided at the chair and at the altar.

The propers are normally those of the day. Afternoon services in places where the propers have been already used in the morning and special or regional confirmation services can employ other sets of readings and prayers.

Parishes want to know what else the bishop is available to do. For instance, might the bishop teach, meet with various groups, or hold a forum? This should be negotiated well in advance.

Bishops should tell parishes the time at which they plan to arrive and then seek to be punctual. Clergy worry when bishops are late; if they arrive at the last minute, many people will be distracted in their worship. As a rule, it is well never to arrive later than 30 minutes before the liturgy. Similarly, too early an arrival gives the rector an additional stressor at an already-tense and busy time. If the bishop plans to meet confirmands, time will need to be adjusted. In some dioceses circumstances permit (or mandate) that the bishop arrive the day before the liturgy, and in this case details concerning arrival at the church can be fine tuned.

Parishes are grateful when bishops tell them what needs to be provided: driving directions, parking, water, a quiet place to center, etc. If bishops have dietary restrictions, it is good to be clear about them (and stick to them no matter how strong may be the temptation to be polite at the expense of one's health).

Vestments and Insignia

The *vestments* of a bishop at full celebrations of confirmation, ordination, or marriage, as at any other eucharist, are an alb, stole, and chasuble. The priests who stand with the bishop at the altar may be similarly vested or else wear alb and stole. The mature western tradition did not enshrine the idea that bishops and priests wear different stoles and the identity of their stoles reflects their collegiality. Additionally, Anglicanism has provided no niche for the pallium, in any sense, although such garments are offered for sale to our bishops by enterprising merchants. In the west the pallium means only one thing: a special participation in the papal ministry by metropolitans, who receive the pallium from Rome. It is similarly hard to imagine a rationale for wearing an eastern-style bishop's stole (the pallium's cousin, the *omophorion*) without its accompanying vestments.[1]

Bishops who wear choir habit (rochet and chimere) for sacramental ministry will have to determine for themselves whether a stole is appropriate over the chimere. Such hybrid use is not what was intended in the evolution of that garment. All other American writers are strongly opposed to the combination, but here it can be recalled in mitigation that the stole worn over the

---

1. In any event, Orthodox vesture also went through a medieval development and does not represent a common ancestor for our vestments in any simple sense; present eastern bishops' regalia represents only sixteenth-century usage. From the opposite point of view, Howard Galley, *The Ceremonies of the Eucharist: A Guide to Celebration* (Cambridge, MA: Cowley Publications, 1989), 207, argues vigorously for the use of one version of the pallium and provides complex instructions for pinning a conventional stole in that shape. The historical information relative to the evolution of vestments is complicated to a degree far beyond the scope of this book, but it can still be observed here that simply choosing an eye-catching depiction from a favored century does not get to the heart of the matter. In the case of the pallium or omophorion, a reading of Paul VI's *motu proprio* of May 11, 1978, *Inter eximia episcopalis*, makes it clear that for an Anglican bishop to appear in an approximation of the pallium would be an occasion of offense (and possibly, derision) to Catholic and protestant alike.

surplice was a gentle transitional stage in many places were there was resistance to the restoration of full vestments; contemporary bishops may also need to chose a middle route in some dioceses.

The *insignia* of a bishop are the mitre, staff, cross, and ring. The mitre and staff are often dispensed with at quiet celebrations on weekdays, but the ring is worn at all times, including Holy Week. The cross is normally worn over the alb and under the chasuble, although it is increasingly seen being worn over plain chasubles. When worn with street clothing, it is tucked into the left breast pocket of shirt or rabat.

The staff is carried in the left hand[2] and is used when entering and leaving the liturgy. The rounded part of the crook faces the people, even when held by an assistant at confirmation and ordination. Additionally, the staff can be held when walking any significant distance during the liturgy, and is held when absolving and blessing. It can also be held (with two hands) during the reading of the gospel. The Feast of the Presentation and Palm Sunday are occasions when the bishop has to carry something else in the left hand, a palm or candle, and at those times alone an assistant carries the staff before the bishop (some prefer that the assistant carry it with the crook facing in on such occasions).

The staff is not a shepherd's crook or even a walking stick in liturgical origin: it came into church life as the staff of office of a Roman official and retains that form to this day in the eastern churches. It evolved, sentimentally but certainly not inappropriately, into something reminiscent of a shepherd's crook in the west alone, but its primary signification is office.[3] Romans and

---

2. To function liturgically one needs to be somewhat ambidextrous because there is plenty for each hand to do; left-right conventions in liturgy are for the sake of all concerned, especially those directly assisting. The connections of the left hand to anything "sinister" are long gone. Good professionalism implies not expecting an entire cast of colleagues to relearn ceremonial conventions because of our own handedness or habits — see the note on vanity, above.

3. In the Roman church, the staff is carried and the mitre is worn by abbots by papal grant, not by right. There is no corresponding Anglican

Anglicans have worried a great deal in the last 125 years about the staff: is it primarily a sign of office or one of jurisdiction? In short, does a bishop carry it in strange territory? The photos of thousands of bishops assembled in Rome, each carrying a staff, may have settled things for that communion (where any bishop may use the staff with the permission of the ordinary). A century ago Percy Dearmer argued in England that the staff ought to be a sign of office and used whenever a bishop presides, but that view has not generally prevailed among Anglicans. When inviting colleagues to preside in their dioceses, bishops should clarify their expectations. At the very least, another bishop ought to carry the staff when representing the diocesan. There is one exception to a rule about local permission: no matter in whose diocese a bishop may be, the staff is always used when presiding at ordination, and is held near the bishop during the ordination rite itself. Bishops probably should acquire a commercially produced stand for the staff because few chancels have convenient places to prop it. It is best not to put the staff on the altar except for the one moment when the new bishop is received in the cathedral and the staff is taken from the altar and solemnly presented.

The mitre is worn in procession and when the bishop is seated. The decorative tabs on the back are called lappets and were originally chin straps. Present-day Anglicans usually wear shorter (eight-to-ten inch) mitres, slightly more ancient in shape than the large Roman and enormous Polish mitres one sees elsewhere.[4] An unornamented mitre, perhaps of plain linen, is expected for Advent, Lent, funerals, and penitential occasions, but it is always appropriate to wear a plain mitre. A bishop uses only one mitre

---

authority able to grant the use of episcopal insignia to abbots in priest's orders. Most Roman scholars and curial reformers would prefer that the practice be suppressed and it has been greatly limited in the last half-decade.

4. Beckett's mitre (1170) is quite short, while the Limerick mitre (1408) is easily twice as tall. It is sufficient to explain this as a matter of changing aesthetics: Freud himself pointed out that sometimes a cigar is just a cigar.

during any liturgy. Mitres are no longer decorated with jewels, and golden mitres are somewhat problematic in all but the largest spaces. In general, mitres have become simpler, and they never need to match other vestments.

Put the mitre on with two hands before taking the staff. It is impossible to put on a mitre symmetrically while holding the staff. Traditionally the mitre may be used, with the staff, to preach, but this is not recommended as a general practice. It is not worn to pray,[5] and is never worn in the presence of the blessed sacrament, including those times when the sacrament is carried in procession. It is not worn during the consecration prayer when ordaining, but may be worn *during the laying-on of hands in confirmation.* It is worn for the anointing and blessing of the sick at public services of healing, but not during the prayers of that liturgy. Ask for or bring a small (perhaps folding) table to be placed near your seat to hold the mitre and other small items: again, the altar is not a good place for either mitre or staff. If the mitre must be placed on the altar for lack of any other place, it should lie flat with the lappets hanging over the side (not front) of the altar.

If you decide to wear a zucchetto (small version of a full skull cap), wear it throughout the liturgy except from the end of the offertory through the clearing of the table. Like the cassock, the zucchetto is an item of haberdashery and not a vestment. The zucchetto is best lined with moleskin because that fabric clings to the head — a consideration especially important for those of us suffering from any degree of alopecia senilis. If one is present in choir habit at a eucharist where others preside and chooses to wear the zucchetto, the head must be bare from the end of the offertory through the clearing of the table.

---

5. Like Mitchell, *Pastoral and Occasional Liturgies* (Cambridge, MA: Cowley Publications, 1998), 106, ff., I believe that too much can be made of this principle; a great deal of donning and doffing the mitre because of the occurrence of brief prayers can lack significance and add distraction.

The chasuble is sufficient for the entire rite. A cope is not worn for the liturgy of the word, confirmation, or ordination when the bishop presiding at those rites is also presiding at the altar in the eucharist. Such change of vesture in the middle of the liturgy serves no positive purpose and may distract the assembly. The only exceptions one can imagine would be those occasions when a procession properly so called is a liturgical unit all its own: Palm Sunday, Candlemas, and Rogationtide come to mind, as do processions with the sacrament immediately following a celebration. The practice of actually celebrating the eucharist in a cope has to do with several peculiarities of the English experience and has nothing to contribute to church life in North America.[6] A well-made cope is just as likely as a chasuble to get wet at baptism, although bishops seldom actually apply the water. If there is a real danger of water damage, any outer vestment being worn should be momentarily laid aside. There are no circumstances when a cope is worn over a chasuble.

At major celebrations and especially at ordinations, some bishops wear a light-weight white dalmatic under the chasuble to symbolize the bishop's identity as source and unity of orders in the diocese, although this practice is not common.

Confirmation is administered sitting or standing, using one or two hands.[7] *At reception into communion*, at least one hand is placed on the candidate's head at the words of blessing. If *chrism* is applied, it is best to apply it at the beginning of the confirmation formula and at the blessing section at the end of the reception formula. If chrism is used for confirmation and reception, there is no reason not to use it at reaffirmation of faith. Immemorial custom notwithstanding, lemon and bread do not effectively remove olive oil any more than butter is good for a burn, so it is well to

---

6. The full-blown Victorian rationalization for this practice may be found in George S. Tyack, *The Historic Dress of the Clergy* (London: Andrews, Hull Press, 1897), 33–35.

7. Rubrics in American prayer books have taken various positions on this question; the present rite says "lays hands," which is subject to a variety of interpretations. Surely two hands are appropriate.

have a *good solvent* handy.[8] Stepping into the sacristy and using soap and water is a possible alternative.

Let the deacon or other clergy of the place handle the offertory and clearing of the altar: they know where things go, and ablution rites seem never to be the same across any diocese.

The clergy of the place appropriately join the bishop at the altar from the eucharistic dialogue through the fraction. This does not necessarily mean *"concelebration"* in the Roman sense, even though the word is commonly used in a broader sense (this subject is treated in detail below).

The bishop should distribute bread, perhaps with other clergy. All of the clergy of the place should join in the administration of Holy Communion. *Lay persons may also assist, as needed, once all the clergy are fulfilling their servant office of feeding.*[9] It is very important for our ecclesiology that the rector and clergy of a parish not "sit out" the eucharist celebrated by the bishop, and it is best to be quite insistent about this. Age, infirmity, or infectious disease may be reasons for the bishop not to distribute. If this is the case, it should be explained to the assembly with appropriate apologies.

Lead the post-communion prayer from chair or altar, depending on the layout of the space, and from that same place give the blessing. The episcopal blessing is given as follows: Put on the mitre and then take the staff. With the staff in the left hand and the right hand over the breast, the bishop begins versicles "Our help is in the name of the Lord, etc." For the blessing itself, raised the right hand, palm out. Three signs of the cross are made

---

8. Canon George Loeffler has developed a special solvent for this purpose. The formula can be obtained by writing him in the care of *bpoffice@diobeth.org*

9. Thus the rubrics of 1979. Some twenty years later a non-binding resolution at General Convention expressed the "mind" that lay people should be ministers of communion regardless of the number of clergy present. This resolution was, in its language and in the speeches endorsing it, unfortunately based in power issues and avoided theological, historical, and sacramental concerns.

with the right hand so as to cover the entire assembly. After the hand is raised, the bishop says, "The blessing, mercy, and grace of God Almighty, the Father [+ left], the Son [+ center], and the Holy Spirit [+ right] be upon you, etc." Some bishops in the Episcopal Church also bless the assembly when walking through it, although this is not common practice and is never to be done from Palm Sunday through the Holy Saturday morning liturgy.

In general, it is wise simply not to do anything that one finds significantly awkward or uncomfortable. It is similarly a mistake to do what one has not practiced. In either case there is a strong possibility that the action will go badly wrong, or not work for the glory of God, or both. People really will understand, especially if the new bishop says that she is not able to do something "yet." The people have thereby been given the gift of the power of tolerating the bishop's finitude or eccentricities.

Finally, the bishop should expect the unexpected, and should try not to lose charity, although composure may sometimes evaporate into that laughter in which the angels join. Fortunately, some ingenuous episcopal pratfalls are permanently endearing. The bishops responding to the survey taken before the writing of this book reported everything from noisily collapsing bishops' chairs to disturbed adults screaming prolonged obscenities during the liturgy. It is also true that the largest number of respondents reported being surprised by how much they were loved and accepted simply because they came in the role of bishop, and how much that fact eclipsed the occasional disaster.

All told, clergy who responded to the survey listed as their first concern that the bishop not come late. The second was that bishops not preach canned confirmation sermons, and third was their hope that bishops not do what makes them uncomfortable.

2. A Basic Guide for Clergy and Congregations

The new bishop will be quite anxious about liturgical ministry for at least a year. She will appreciate your understanding and support in this learning time, and throughout the episcopate.

If not elected from within the diocese, the new bishop will be trying to establish relationships and detect the lay of the land during the first year or so. Consequently, the bishop may regrettably avoid clarity about preferences, and parish leaders may have to pry out some details if the liturgy is to go smoothly.

An affable "do what you usually do" is an answer of limited usefulness, as this liturgy is not the "usual" celebration, so it is well to be sure to go over things carefully with the bishop or the bishop's assistant. At the very least, there should be understanding about entrance and exit rites, who sits where, who helps with hat and staff, what happens at the peace, offertory, communion, and closing rites.

A brand-new bishop may not realize that each parish has variations on what happens around the fraction and preparation of vessels in particular. It is best to ask the bishop to take a step back and stand perfectly still after the fraction and let local people prepare the vessels for distribution. There is no consistency across the church about what is said or sung at the fraction, so do not fear briefing the bishop in detail. During the announcements it is more appropriate to "greet" than to "welcome" the bishop (and spouse), as the bishop is in fact the chief pastor of the parish.

At all visitations the rector or person in charge should greet the bishop at the entrance or parking lot and escort the bishop into the church. This duty of greeting by the rector is not to be delegated, as it is a function of both collegiality and hospitality for the head of the house to greet the one who is in some respects a guest. Give the bishop a decent, quiet, and private place to vest and otherwise prepare for the liturgy. The newer the bishop the more important this consideration is.

Bishops, because they usually preside, preach, and administer other rites during the liturgy, will have a strain on their voices. Glasses of cold water should be placed where the bishop can conveniently reach them.

If the bishop does not travel with a deacon or other chaplain, have at least one quick-witted *adult* trained to assist so that the bishop has help with mitre and staff during the liturgy and does not have to remember where they were put down. This assistant should practice handing the bishop the mitre so that it goes on forwards, and should always place the staff in the bishop's left hand. I remain unconvinced that separate assistants are always needed for mitre and staff (at ordination this is useful because other items must also be handled), although this is the requirement of the Roman rite and recommended by some contemporary Anglican writers.

No matter what the normal liturgical style of a place may be, when the bishop comes the liturgy is going to be relatively complex, especially if it involves baptism, confirmation, reception, or reaffirmation. It is accordingly very important to rehearse all concerned quite thoroughly; rehearsal dispels nervousness on the part of candidates and aids everyone in entering the experience with a worshiping attitude. After careful consideration of the layout of your church, leaders should propose a plan to the bishop regarding where candidates, sponsors, and others stand for the various parts of the rite. Failing to rehearse candidates for baptism or other initiatory rites in their responses and movements does a great disservice to all concerned.

Ideally, the usual place of liturgical presidency should suffice for presiding at baptism, confirmation, and related rites. Given the layout of our churches, this is almost never the case. If the bishop does not bring a *faldstool* (liturgical folding camp chair) and there are many candidates, a chair for the bishop is placed where people can see and where candidates have a place to kneel. Older prayer books prescribed that this be directly in front of the altar, but the real question is one of sight-lines. If the bishop prefers to confirm standing, and there are no adult baptisms, receptions, or reaffirmation, the bishop may choose to have people kneel at the altar rail. (This is not recommended on both theoretical and practical grounds, however, as will be explained below.)

Musicians will want to find out if the bishop needs pitches for sung portions of the service, and whether the bishop prefers a single pitch or an incipit. If the episcopal blessing is to be used and the entire service is not printed out, the service folder should print it out or else ensure that people know where to find it (*The Hymnal 1982*, S-173). The bishop will put on the mitre and take the staff before beginning the blessing.

There must be perfect clarity with the bishop about when the dismissal comes in relation to the blessing and final music. It helps to find out if the bishop would like to be relieved of the staff and mitre when greeting people at the door after the liturgy.

It is best to instruct the congregation not to take photographs during the liturgy. It is spiritually important that the liturgy be an experience of worship at the very moment of its celebration and not an "event" to be savored later. Inform people that you will hold the candidates in their places after the liturgy so that group and individual pictures can be taken with the bishop.

The rector or other lay leaders should make sure the bishop is aware of what is new, exciting, or challenging in the life of the parish well before the visitation. The bishop should ordinarily initiate this conversation, but if the pressure of newness prevents this, parish leadership should not hesitate to start the communication.

CHAPTER THREE

The Parish Visitation
with a Note on Eucharists at Which the Bishop Does Not Preside at the Altar

The majority of responding bishops and clergy do not recommend regional confirmations as a regular practice. Some bishops have instituted them to unify the diocese and report good results. However, a few have done so out of a kind of frustration with which it is not hard to sympathize. Every year when the visitation schedule goes out, in diocese upon diocese, somebody genuinely intending to be kind calls the bishop's secretary and asks to be taken off the visitation list. "The bishop shouldn't go to the trouble of driving up here to visit — we don't have anybody to be confirmed." The hope of the bishops who regularly confirm regionally is that the parish visitation will be events of pastoral and missional depth, from which initiation could serve as a distraction. The canons seem to assume initiation as part of the visit, however.

Thus it is well to teach often and clearly about the nature of visitation. Two relevant sections of the Canons are worth repeating here.

Canons (2003) III.18.3

...Each Diocesan Bishop shall visit the Congregations within the Diocese at least once in three years. Interim visits may be delegated to another Bishop of this Church.

(b) At every visitation the visiting Bishop shall preside at the Holy Eucharist and at the Initiatory Rites, as required,

24

preach the Word, examine the records of the Congregation required by Canon III.9.5(c), and examine the life and ministry of the Clergy and Congregation according to Canon III.9.5(b)(5).

The parish and priest's duties are reciprocal and quite specific:

III.9.5

(5) On notice being received of the Bishop's intention to visit any congregation, the Rector shall announce the fact to the congregation. At every visitation it shall be the duty of the Rector and the Wardens, Vestry or other officers, to exhibit to the Bishop the Parish Register and to give information as to the state of the congregation, spiritual and temporal, in such categories as the Bishop shall have previously requested in writing.

I take this to mean that visitation is inquiry, conversation, celebration, and encouragement. Inquiry means getting the facts that the canons require and helping the congregation assess itself against its own mission statement and commitment as a member of the larger Church. As time goes on the bishop learns to listen through the cracks of conversation, especially as to what is not said. Sometimes direct questions about ministry and mission will cause other issues to surface (often as reasons why mission is not being undertaken). One of the delights for me has been to discover the extent to which even the smallest of parishes participates in outreach ministry and supports our diocesan work in Africa. These things need to be celebrated; I routinely tell children that it is my job to go from place to place encouraging Jesus' sisters and brothers. Bishops' not unnatural problem-solving orientation needs to be supplemented, if not supplanted, by the celebration and encouragement aspects of the visitation.

It is difficult to make all of this happen on a Sunday morning, and it is even less likely to happen on a Sunday afternoon. For the last four years the Diocese of Bethlehem has followed a different pattern. As is true elsewhere, it is our tradition that "*episcope* is exercised in community," and the entire staff of Diocesan House is in mission to the diocese. In this context it has worked well to break the visitation down into parts. About two weeks before the bishop visits, the archdeacon (sometimes with another member of the staff) appears at a non-optional open meeting with parish leaders to review the finances, physical structure, and strategies for mission in the parish. This follows the syllabus as described in the canons. The inquiries are quite specific. Because no one need hurry home to a confirmation party, this meeting becomes a time for serious conversation. Sometimes that is a subject of joy, and on other occasions it has opened up difficult issues that have been neglected or denied for years. On one occasion, in getting ready for the archdeacon's visit, a parish discovered $40,000 it had forgotten it had and used it as seed money for a medical clinic.

The archdeacon discusses the results of the preliminary visit with the bishop (and sometimes the entire staff). Necessary follow-up is planned using whatever resources are needed, and thus the bishop has a pastoral context in which to preach and engage in conversation with parishioners and leaders at the Sunday visit.

Under these circumstances, when the bishop arrives it is not to make a general speech or deliver a standard confirmation sermon. Rather, the bishop can feel like and function as the chief pastor of the place with a relevant word from the day's lessons, and is prepared to engage the congregation at a meeting with significant objectives. It is also good to meet with vestry and other leaders after the general meeting. Discovering who the real leaders, validators, and gate-keepers are in a parish requires good ears.

The foregoing solution to the visitation question is not proposed as a model anyone else needs to use, but demonstrates the way one bishop has tried to help people perceive the visitation as a pastoral act of scope far exceeding the celebration of confirmation.

Preparing for the Visitation Liturgy

The visitation schedule is usually prepared in the late spring to allow people time to trade dates or make necessary changes. The schedule is mailed with the current version of the customary for visitations. About six weeks before the visitation, the bishop's office sends a form for the rector to complete. It asks for the time of service, what initiatory rites (if any) will be celebrated, the rite used for the eucharist, and the color being used. It asks for parking details and what meetings are scheduled with the parish, vestry, and other groups. It asks if there are special events or concerns the bishop should have in mind when planning the sermon.

Such an information form may appear naïve and basic, but together with the detailed service information, and the archdeacon's visit, it provides the bishop with a good deal of data — especially if the secretary or chaplain needs to hound the rector or other leadership to get it.

Parishes need to be reminded that the prayer book expects that baptisms planned for any occasions at all near the time of the bishop's visit be reserved for the visit. It is a matter of considerable regret that this norm is widely neglected.

For morning visitations the proper of the day is always used, while in afternoon liturgies where there has already been a morning service, the propers might be those of confirmation, or baptism, or another occasion. The importance of the bishop's modeling good preaching on the lessons of the day cannot be overemphasized. Without exception, priest and deacon respondents to my inquiries expressed pronounced discomfort with canned confirmation sermons. The clergy and people of the place need to hear the bishop engage the readings that shape the church's life, and the bishop needs to be one with the parochial clergy who week by week labor to preach the scriptures.

It is worth the bishop's emphasizing to liturgically adventurous rectors that the appearance of the bishop is not be the time to do things that the majority of the congregation does not care for. It is not helpful for the bishop's relationship to the congregation to have strange practices endured because "the bishop wants this," when that is not true. In a prophylactic sense, it is well for the bishop to let the diocese know often and clearly that the bishop has no intention of regulating local liturgical details not addressed in the rubrics. Incense, choices of posture, alternative texts, and methods of communion distribution come to mind as issues where rectors have blamed the bishop for their own innovations.

The Bishop's Chaplain

Nothing I did liturgically in my early episcopate got more thanks from clergy and congregations than did assigning one of our deacons as my chaplain. He is a person they can easily contact with questions about liturgical celebration, seating details, how to prepare the space, and other practical matters, and clergy referred to his existence as a stress-reducer for them. He prepares all liturgical material for the bishop, and arrives about an hour before I do to deal with any last-minute questions in the parish and make sure all is ready. He is not my driver, nor does he keep my date book, although he does bring some equipment. He knows episcopal ceremonial thoroughly and saves local clergy from having to master details or train someone in the parish to function self-consciously as pick-up assistant to the bishop in the liturgy. Because he is a deacon, he also exposes parishioners who otherwise do not see deacons to that order of ministry. In parishes where there already is a deacon, he serves only as my chaplain, and leaves all other diaconal functions to the deacon of the place.

The Visitation Liturgy

The following schema assumes a eucharist containing the celebration of baptism, confirmation, and reception. This liturgical schema, minus the initiatory material, is the basic pattern for all of the bishop's public celebrations ("stational" liturgies).

Items to Have Ready

In your car

- vestments
- staff and mitre
- chrism, if the bishop brings it
- in the early days, it is well to check that one has remembered to wear the ring and pectoral cross before setting out. Keep extra collars, collar buttons or tab collars in the car, along with hairbrush and mouthwash. If you (are a man who) cannot sew a button, it is good to learn and to carry a sewing kit.

In the chancel

- the altar book (or authorized supplemental texts)
- prayer book and hymnal at the bishop's place (even if the liturgy is printed out, the prayer book may be needed)
- the lectionary at the reading desk
- the prayers for the candidates, together with the prayers of the people, with local petitions, either at the reading desk or in the hands of the person who will lead those prayers
- vessels for the eucharist, together with sufficient linens

At the place where the bishop will sit for the initiatory rites

- chrism and solvent, if used

In the nave

- bread, wine (and water) for the eucharist
- plates or baskets for collecting other offerings

At the font

- the paschal candle
- other candles if they are to be given in baptism

In the sacristy or vesting room

- the book of the gospels
- censer and incense boat, if used
- processional cross — one is sufficient for all liturgies of any size
- two or more torches

Vestments are the color of the day. Some bishops permit the optional use of white or red when initiatory rites are celebrated and the color is otherwise green. From Advent through the Lord's Baptism, and from Ash Wednesday through the day of Pentecost the color of the day is used without exception.

Entrance

If incense is used, the bishop places incense on the coals, and blesses it silently.

The procession enters in this order:

[thurifer]

crucifer carrying cross, image facing forward

torches

[choir]

liturgical assistants

deacons who will not be assisting

priests who will not be at the altar

deacon with gospel book

priests who will be at the altar

the bishop's chaplain/deacon

the bishop, with staff and mitre

[two deacons]

The procession could be larger in some circumstances. Ideally the bishop would be preceded and followed by deacons, but in all but the largest liturgies this is impossible. A growing number of parishes employ the services of vergers who act in some ways as master of ceremonies and liturgical factotum. The verger would enter before the thurifer.

The clergy reverence the altar with a bow from the waist and go to their places. The bishop arrives at the altar, hands the staff and mitre to those assisting, and bows from the waist. From the practical standpoint, this profound bow is not possible with the mitre on, but the intent of removing the mitre is reverence. When it is the custom, the bishop kisses the altar before going to the place where opening rites will be led. In places where incense is used, the bishop censes the altar now or during the Gloria in Excelsis, if it is sung.

The bishop does not separate the opening hymn from the text of the liturgy with personal comments or greetings. To do so would be to destroy the "gathering" function of prelude, bells, and hymn. The sermon and announcement time are excellent for such greetings.

Ideally the bishop presides at the opening rites and liturgy of the word from the normal place of presidency in the church, facing the people. This is often directly behind the altar or to the side of the altar. Presbyters sit with the bishop as colleagues, as far as the space permits. Deacons and liturgical assistants do not sit with the bishop as colleagues, but sit or stand nearby, ready to assist.

Since the late nineteenth century, many Episcopal churches are arranged with a "bishop's chair" inside the sanctuary rail; these chairs are often situated in places that are not ideal in the contemporary liturgical climate. Because the liturgy of the word is increasingly celebrated from a place outside the sanctuary rail (and indeed, the altar actually to be used may be outside that rail), a dilemma can arise. Many parishes with immoveable bishop's chairs hope for their use, and while it may not be liturgically ideal, it is polite to use them. Crucifers sometimes are unaccustomed to anyone entering the sanctuary during the entrance rite and may have to be reminded to make room for the bishop and assistants to pass. If the bishop's chair is entirely out of sight, it is well to lead the opening rite from before the chancel opening, in front of the altar, or at some other convenient spot where the bishop may be both seen and heard by all. A disembodied voice coming over a public address system with no visible source is unedifying and certainly does not gather the attention and energy of the congregation, as an entrance rite is intended to do.

At the usual place of presidency or in another place visible to all, the bishop, without staff or mitre, makes the sign of the cross and says or sings the opening acclamation (BCP, p. 299). After the brief dialogue, the Gloria in Excelsis may be sung and the altar censed, if this was not done during the entrance hymn. The prayer book favors omitting the Gloria when initiation is celebrated, apparently to save time, but the festivity of the occasion, especially if baptism is being celebrated, argues in favor of using it or another canticle.

The bishop faces the people and says or sings the salutation and collect. The bishop sits and puts on the mitre. The lessons are read.

During the time that the gradual hymn or other music is being sung the bishop sits to charge and bless the thurible. Then the deacon or priest who is to read the gospel takes the gospel book and bows or kneels before the bishop, asking for a blessing. If the bishop was standing for the hymn and has not already taken a seat to bless incense, she sits at this point. The bishop says, "The Lord be in your heart and on your lips that you may worthily and competently proclaim his gospel. In the name of the Father...," making the sign of the cross. This bit of ceremony, as that which follows, emphasizes the bishop's primary responsibility for the proclamation of the good news of Jesus. When all have been deployed for the reading, the bishop removes the mitre, stands, and takes the staff with both hands. As the reader of the Gospel arrives in place (with or without procession), the bishop along with the assembly faces the reader. After the reading, the book is brought to the bishop, who may venerate it with a kiss.

The bishop preaches the sermon. At baptism, the rubric permits the sermon to be preached after the peace. This is to provide for "mystagogical catechesis," an exposition of the baptismal rite to those who have just undergone it. As part of a parish visitation this practice is not preferable because the homiletical connection to the lessons of the day and the overall mission needs to be of a piece with the proclamation of the readings. The sermon should address parish concerns and should include words to the candidates, but its center is ordinarily the day's scriptures.

If no initiatory rites are celebrated, the bishop returns to the chair and begins the creed. The bishop says the collect at the end of the prayers of the people, the absolution, and the peace.

When there is initiation, after the sermon the bishop goes to the place where a seat has been prepared in the sight of all for the presentation and examination of candidates (BCP, p. 301) The bishop sits and puts on the mitre. The staff may be held nearby.

It is a liturgical commonplace that "the space always wins," and in a large celebration of Christian initiation this is especially true. Ideally, all candidates and their sponsors and presenters should come forward, be presented, and remain in a group in front of the bishop through the baptismal covenant. Working with the rectors, the bishop will need to establish a pattern that works in each place.

Adult candidates for baptism, infant candidates, candidates for confirmation, those for reception, and finally those who are making reaffirmation of baptismal vows are presented. The bishop sits through the baptismal covenant as an expression of presidency, quite literally chairing the meeting, to be sure, and as one ages and the churches grow, the practical considerations for sitting increase.

The bishop stands and removes the mitre for the prayers for the candidates. These prayers, on Sunday, may well be followed without pause by intercessions and thanksgivings appropriate to the place and time. The bishop then says the concluding collect.

Presentation and examination of candidates

In some places prayers for the candidates will be sung in procession to the font, in which case the mitre is worn. The bishop blesses the font, bare-headed. The bishop blesses chrism at this moment, if necessary, although the blessing of chrism is normally an annual diocesan event. The bishop resumes the mitre. Ordinarily local clergy administer the water of baptism in accordance with ancient tradition and their pastoral relationship with the candidates and families they have prepared.

In the reconstruction of liturgical origins on which the present prayer book initiatory rite was based, reformers imagined an ancient scenario in which the water baptism took place in a room separate from that where the assembly was gathered (for practical reasons as well as those of modesty). The baptized were taken into the assembly and presented to the bishop in the sight of all for a final blessing and the peace. Later developments in a variety of post-baptismal anointings together with the blessing and embrace form the origin of what has come to be called the rite of confirmation. The embrace shrank to a touch, and finally mutated into a little slap. With the restoration of the peace, the slap has no purpose.

In memory of all this, after all are baptized, nowadays the bishop returns to the seat in front of the assembly. The newly baptized (they or their sponsors/parents bearing their candles) are brought as a group before the bishop. The bishop stands without the mitre and prays over them as a group (BCP, p. 308). The bishop sits and receives the mitre. One by one the newly baptized are brought before the bishop. Those able to kneel do so. Using a thumb, the bishop applies chrism, lays on hands and says, "You are sealed. . . . " Rubrics permit alteration of this sequence, but when the rite is performed in this way, it becomes ritually clear that the subsequent confirmation of those baptized as adults when the bishop is present to lay on hands at baptism is entirely superfluous.

Neophytes remain near the bishop after the laying-on of hands until that action has been completed for all the baptized. Then all of them face the congregation and the bishop begins the welcome.

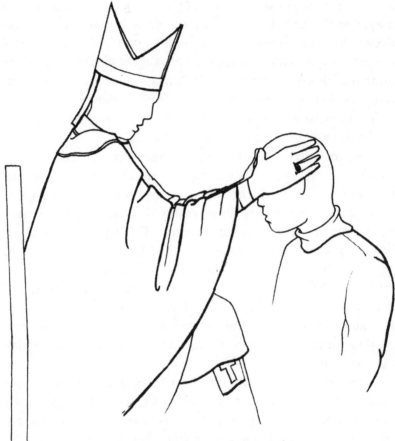

Anointing of the newly baptized

The carrying of infants through the congregation by priests or bishop during the welcome should be avoided. This practice is unhelpful because it focuses on the clergy as sentimentally child-friendly, distracts from the life-and-death quality of the rite, and is entirely disrespectful of those adults who have in their baptism made the perhaps courageous decision to follow Christ and are now left standing like extras at the front of the church while all beam at the babies.

The neophytes and their sponsors either stand to the side, or if there is no room, take their seats. Those to be confirmed or received, and those who are to make reaffirmation, stand before the bishop, who without the mitre says the prayer on page 309. The bishop sits and takes the mitre. Candidates are brought to the bishop one by one. As evangelism takes root in the Episcopal Church and we increasingly see dozens if not hundreds of confirmands at each service, the practicality of sitting to confirm will become clear, although sitting remains primarily an expression of presidency.

As has been mentioned, confirmation has its origins in a small greeting and blessing. Aidan Kavanagh has demonstrated that this little action emphasized the engrafting of the neophytes into the congregation of the faithful and also dismissed or "deployed" them as members of Christ's task force in the world.[1] Only later did the long and complicated history of this action as a separate rite, finally a separate sacrament, begin, and we cannot dwell on that discussion here. It is enough to say that hints of two developed traditions coexist in the 1979 rite, Catholic and protestant.[2] The rite tries to honor the Reformation emphasis on education, formation, and personal acceptance of the baptismal relationship. It also maintains room for the developed western concept of a blessing for spiritual strength. The present text carefully avoids saying that the confirmands are doing the confirming (Lutheran) or that the bishop is "conferring" the Holy Spirit (Cyprian), although the rite provides a way to honor one or both beliefs by those who hold them.

Chrismation, a recent restoration to Anglican liturgical life, is a repeatable rite in the east, although it is not always recalled that among the Orthodox it is not casually or routinely repeated. In view of confirmation's labyrinthine history and uncertain theology, it is enough to say that as a sign of each baptized person's identity with *messiach* it is permissible to chrismate whenever

---

1. Aidan Kavanagh, *Confirmation* (New York: Pueblo, 1988).
2. The writer who best explains the genesis and ambiguities of the 1970 rite is Leonel Mitchell, *Praying Shapes Believing* (Harrisburg, PA: Morehouse, 1991).

baptismal vows are solemnly renewed before the bishop. It follows that chrism should be used for confirmation, reception, and
reaffirmation alike.

Energy is consumed by writers as to whether or not the mitre is
worn for confirmation and whether the bishop sits. As Mitchell,
who prefers the mitre's omission, agrees, its use at this moment
is permissible, given the symbolic nature of the mitre as sign of
the presence of the larger church in the person of the bishop.
Galley, however, makes much more of this brief prayer and blessing than do Kavanagh and I.[3] He sees the prayer and blessing in
terms very much as solemn as ordination, and tunes ceremonial
accordingly, shifting the weight of the confirmation liturgy from
the profession of faith to the bishop's gift. More convincing to me
is the contrary argument that unlike the ordination prayer, which
is a solemn prayer shaped like the eucharistic prayers, this little
blessing is a relatively modest act not to be confused with the
solemnities of either baptism or ordination. The dangerous assertion of a previous generation that confirmation is an "ordination
to the apostolate of the laity," that lurks behind Galley's assertion,
does great damage in that it takes the clerical state as the norm,
a concept that our present baptismal theology cannot support.
Consequently the ritual distinction between confirmation and ordination should be strongly drawn, and this distinction is aided
by the posture and costume of the bishop, who sits and wears
the mitre. This decision also keeps weight equally distributed
between the candidate's profession of faith and commitment to
discipleship on the one hand and the bishop's act on the other.

For reception, the candidate kneels and the bishop takes the
candidate's right hand in the bishop's left hand, covering it with
the bishop's right. The bishop then says, "We recognize you . . .
fellowship of this communion" (BCP, p. 310). Continuing to
hold the candidate's right hand in the bishop's left, the bishop
anoints the forehead with the right thumb and lays on the right

---

3. Galley, *The Ceremonies of the Eucharist*, 221.

hand for the little formula of blessing. This somewhat complicated procedure solves several theoretical problems, chief of which is that every denomination defines confirmation differently. Roman Catholics who come for reception have usually not made a "mature public profession" of faith before a bishop, yet believe themselves to be confirmed. Lutherans have not received the laying-on of episcopal hands at their (usually adolescent) confirmations. Orthodox usually have done neither. Many protestants, who emphasize their previous profession of faith, do sometimes insist on being received rather than confirmed. The procedure just outlined, by combining hands with the blessing, should satisfy the sensibilities of all while not forcing people into a death-duel over terminology that may be breathing its last.

Those making a reaffirmation kneel, are chrismated, and are blessed with the laying-on of a hand.

The bishop then prays over the entire group of those confirmed, received, and making reaffirmation, standing, without the mitre, which is resumed for the peace. If necessary, the baptismal party is brought back before the bishop with the other candidates, and the peace is exchanged. The bishop should have reasonable opportunity to greet all candidates before they return to greet family and friends, but as numbers swell in the church, this may not be a possibility.

Whom and how many people to greet at the peace during any eucharist remains problematic. Clearly in small groups it is possible for everyone to greet each member of the assembly fairly quickly. As numbers grow this becomes impossible. What is meant to be an expression of *God's* peace as our access to the altar and bond with each other, has become in some places a celebration of our good will, and in others a preliminary coffee hour.

Surely in our culture any celebration of good will is not a bad thing. However, it is God's peace we express, and sharing the eucharist is the highest experience of our connection with each other in Christ. When the passing of peace takes longer than the eucharistic prayer and, in some places, is as long as the communion rite, proportionality is lost. At the same time, having too-explicit rules, such as a rule that one should only greet those whom one can reach without moving from one's place, seems severe. Perhaps before the peace reaches half the length of the eucharistic prayer of that day, it should end. On the other hand, I was present with Sudanese refugees in church in Kampala at the moment of the signing of the peace treaty that ended almost fifty years of civil war. It would have been impossible to contain the peace on that occasion, so all I argue for here is a sense of what I have called proportionality, including proportionality of occasion. The bishop who makes a point of greeting every member of an assembly numbering more than a handful may, like baby-carrying rectors, be diverting attention from a ritual moment to her own affability. On more general principles, if one is going to greet each person at the door, doing so at the peace as well seems over the top.

Any chair that was set up for the initiatory rites is cleared during the sharing of peace, and the bishop goes to the seat from which she presided at the liturgy of the word. It is not uncommon for rectors to make announcements and greet the bishop (and the bishop's spouse). The bishop says the offertory sentence, if any, and sits.

If a bishop travels with a deacon or other chaplain, that person can make sure that whatever the offertory practices of the parish may be, the vessels end up in places where the bishop can gracefully reach them during the Great Thanksgiving. It is better to have this done before the bishop reaches the altar, in preference to the bishop reaching the altar and rearranging things. Failing all this, preferences can be made known to the assisting clergy. Most bishops prefer a single chalice on the altar (as recommended but not required in the rubrics), aligned side-by-side with the container of bread. The chalice should be on the right, so that the deacon can more easily reach it for the final elevation. "Real bread" is any baked mixture of wheat flour and water, and energy is not helpfully expended on the subject.

When the altar is completely prepared the bishop approaches it. If the bishop has not done so earlier, and it is her practice, the offertory is a moment to venerate the altar with a kiss.

In churches where incense is used only once, it will be at the offertory. The bishop will be presented with the thurible, which is charged and blessed. Circles and crosses are no longer made over the gifts, so the censing is quite simple for the beginner. Three swings of the thurible, center, left, right, in the direction of the gifts will do. Swings with the thurible may be doubled. Then the bishop walks around the altar, censing it on the way. It is not necessary to cense candlesticks and crosses, although that is not inappropriate.

After the censing, the bishop returns to the center of the altar and hands the thurible to the deacon. Bows from the neck are exchanged, and the deacon censes the bishop, followed by bows. The deacon censes the other clergy and the people (in some places the thurifer does this).

The bishop and the priests joining the bishop at the altar wash their hands. The priests take their places on either side of the bishop. The deacon stands a little behind the bishop, to the right. If only one priest is with the bishop, that priest stands to the left of the bishop.

The Puzzle of "Concelebration"

There came a problem with the laudable Roman Catholic decision that the ancient norm of one mass in the community was preferable to the practices of twenty priests simultaneously saying twenty masses in tiny chapels with one or no assistant. (We must admit that this deplorable situation crept into parts of Anglicanism, even in North America). With this decision in favor of one mass at one altar many Roman clergy perceived a threat to a priestly spirituality that centered in the daily offering of mass by each priest. This concern was accompanied by the practical question of the stipends that had been offered for priests to remember particular intentions when celebrating. Perceived necessity can be the mother of evolution. Although some Roman liturgiologists objected, the ancient evidence of priests standing together with their bishop (which by the middle ages occurred only at ordination) and the contemporary eastern practice of presbyters standing together at the altar were taken to support the idea that priests could, even though standing together at one altar, all exercise sacerdotal power and individual "intentions" during one and the same mass. It is not my place or desire to criticize that decision here, as our tradition shares almost none of its foundational beliefs, but rather to explain how the notion of "concelebration" suddenly got into the air at the time when prayer books were being reformed in Anglicanism.

Following the very same ancient evidence, but construing it more strictly, the 1979 prayer book says very simply, "It is appropriate that the other priests present stand with the celebrant at the Altar, and join in the consecration of the gifts, in breaking the Bread, and in distributing Communion" (p. 354). This position is closer to the Orthodox thought and practice than to the Roman and is intended to be an expression of collegiality in the stewardship of the mysteries, a stewardship with which they are entrusted by the church at ordination for the sake of all Christians. No time is more appropriate for the expression of this concept than the occasion when bishop and presbyters are together.

It is best not to have joint recitation of the eucharistic prayer, particularly the institution narrative or concluding doxology. The following outline may serve (see pages 63–67 for illustrations).

PRAYER A, and similarly for B, D[4]

At the dialogue through the preface, only the bishop assumes the orans position. All others stand with hands joined before the breast.

---

4. Prayer C's shape and dialogical form probably make it unsuitable for the kind of celebration described here. If it is employed, the order of the actions for the invocation of the Holy Spirit and the oblation must be reversed.

At the Sanctus, all bow from the waist with the bishop through the words "heaven and earth are fully of your glory."

As the post-Sanctus portion of the prayer begins, all assume the orans position.

When the bishop begins the institution narrative, those standing with the bishop join their hands again. At the word concerning the bread and again at that concerning the cup, they extend the right hand, palm up, and then rejoin their hands at the end of each passage.

At the memorial all open their hands again. While the bishop indicates the elements at the words "we offer you these gifts" those standing at the altar continue to hold their hands open.

When the bishop joins her hands following the oblation, all those standing by do so as well.

At the invocation of the Holy Spirit the bishop (may make the sign of the cross and) extend hands over the elements; those standing by extend the right hand, palm down.

All join the bishop in signing themselves with the cross at "Sanctify us also ...," and extend their hands again.

At the words "your Son, Jesus Christ" they join their hands and keep them joined as the bishop and deacon elevate the bread the cup, holding them up through the people's Amen. The bishop holds up the bread, and the deacon, with two hands, holds the cup at the height of the bishop's shoulders.

All bow from the waist after the Amen.

Communion Rite

The Lord's Prayer is said or sung, the bishop's hands open.

The bread is broken, silence is observed, and the fraction anthem is said or sung. Each rector/organist team has a pattern

regarding how the silence is observed, and it usually errs on the
side of brevity or else the silence is ignored entirely. If the bishop
prefers silence lasting more than the blink of an eye, it is often
necessary to clarify expectations with the organist directly. The
text of the fraction anthem, especially with regard to its length,
should be sufficient to cover the preparation of all vessels but not
go much longer. The preparation of vessels is a purely utilitar-
ian act and should be completed with dispatch. Fraction anthems
such as Agnus Dei entered the liturgy only as a covering for the
preparation of vessels, and do not by design carry devotional significance that would interfere with smooth preparation for the
distribution of Holy Communion.

The bishop takes the consecrated elements first. In the ancient
(and contemporary) east, where our sacred meal arises, the host
first takes the food and drink at all meals to indicate that the
food is good and now to be shared by all. This is not so foreign
a concept: at a dinner party in our culture nobody begins to eat
until the hostess or host first lifts a fork. The reception of Holy
Communion by the president is a sign of hospitality, quality of
food, and the beginning of the meal; however, no one need stare
in rapt attention as the president and others at the altar receive
communion. In fact, after the one presiding has begun to receive,
people might well begin lining up to share in the holy gifts.

The communion of other ministers and assistants at the altar
ought not be a prolonged ceremonial moment either, and given
the constraints of the space, should be done with dispatch. Certainly in large churches where communion is given at stations, a
way can be found to communicate choirs and others who may be
in the chancel while distribution has begun in the nave.

The bishop goes to the chair until the altar is cleared and all is
ready for the post-communion prayer. The layout of the room and
practices of the place will determine whether or not this prayer
is said at the altar. The chair, if well situated, is a good place for
both the post-communion prayer and the blessing.

Ordination as priest or bishop includes the obligation "to pronounce God's blessing" (BCP, p. 531), but in the last forty years

some confusion has arisen over the function of liturgical blessing. A final blessing was not really wanted in the 1979 book, although it was tolerated as an option, but no text was given, despite millennia of practice. One must look in the ordination rites of the prayer book just to locate blessing texts.

This situation is changing. The post-1979 addition of seasonal blessings has reopened the door of holy imagination in the matter of blessing, and the *Enriching Our Worship* series has expanded the horizons of blessing language considerably.

In catechesis, the bishop has the opportunity to remind people that biblically, blessing makes someone or something holy, that is, devoted to God. Thus our new perception of the person, thing, or relationship blessed provides it with a new "set apart" identity and gives it focused purpose. Additionally, along with our varying understanding of how God acts in history, we pray for preservation for people, things, and relationships because that is our heart's desire, and needs to be brought to God. The primary meaning is holiness; good fortune is an overlay.

For the chief pastor of a community to conclude its assembly with this creative and sanctifying word of God's intention, of God's perception of the people, has long been understood as an essential part of episcopal liturgy. It certainly expresses the bishop's love for the people and her appreciation for the relationship God has given them. That some people will perceive the blessing as a species of luck is unavoidable; that most will increasingly understand themselves beloved of God is at least as likely.

During the times for which there is a seasonal blessing in *The Book of Occasional Services*, those blessings might be used. There is nonetheless something to be said for using the episcopal blessing most of the time, as it can become a way of intensifying awareness of the loving bond between bishop and diocese. In Lent it is best to use the "Prayers over the People" found among the seasonal blessings.

As previously described, the episcopal blessing begins with the taking of mitre and staff. The prayer book does not contemplate the insertion of a hymn between blessing and dismissal, but this does not seem to be a battle that can be won in all places. The dismissal should be said facing the people.

"Coram Episcopo" — *When the Bishop Does not Preside at the Altar*

Coram Episcopo means "in the presence of the bishop," and is the name for various sets of ceremonial directions for eucharists at which the bishop is vested and in the chair, but at which the bishop does not preside at the altar. A bishop merely sitting in the pews is not liturgically present and thus has no liturgical responsibilities, although in practice may be asked to come forward and give a blessing, a liturgically irregular but pleasant occasion.

For most bishops, it is only physical infirmity or contagion that will prevent presidency at the visitation eucharist. Those occasions do occur, so what follows is the most simplified version of the tradition possible. There are also moments when a bishop will ask a priest to preside. Ordination anniversaries, retirements, and family events come to mind in this regard.

On these occasions the bishop vests in stole, cope, and mitre, and carries the staff. If fully ambulatory, the bishop takes the usual place at the end of the procession. After removing the mitre and reverencing the altar, she goes to her place. The bishop says the opening acclamation and presides through the peace. If the place is one where water is blessed at the offertory, the priest presiding at the altar blesses the water and the incense. The bishop is incensed after the priest presiding at the altar. The bishop remains at the chair (unless it does not provide visual access to the altar) for the eucharistic prayer, and adopts the same posture as other worshipers. The bishop receives communion after the priest presiding at the altar. The bishop may be seated during the distribution to the assembly, remaining bareheaded. After the post-communion prayer, the bishop blesses the people.

If this is still too much, and an infirm bishop simply must be present, it is enough that the bishop give the (absolution and) blessing, other clergy presiding at the liturgy of the word.

It sometimes happens that another bishop will be invited to preside while the diocesan bishop is vested and seated in the cathedra. If for some reason the two bishops are not to stand at the altar together, it is appropriate for the diocesan to participate only by giving the blessing, and even this may be ceded to the visitor. Ordinarily the diocesan would carry the staff. When the Presiding Bishop is present at a diocesan celebration where the bishop of the diocese is present, the primatial cross is carried by or before the primate and the diocesan carries the staff. The primate is given the place of honor in the procession and follows the diocesan, with the usual deacons in attendance.

The prayer book rubrics for marriage and burial provide for partial presidency by the bishop at those events, and they are examined in Chapter Seven.

CHAPTER FOUR

The Cathedral Ordination of Presbyters
with the Reception of the Orders
of One Previously Ordained,
and a Brief Note on the Ordination of Deacons

Many moments in episcopal ministry both thrill and humble, and surely ordination is high on anyone's list. Presiding at ordination as candidates are entrusted with a ministry to which the bishop's own life has been given will bring many emotions to the surface. It is therefore quite important that the new bishop thoroughly practice the ordination rite aloud in private in order to deal with and master those emotions, so that the liturgy may flow as intended.

Every ordination is entry into a collegial office, and this is most obvious in the case of the ordination of presbyters. It is also to be observed that the ordained serve a diocese as well as a parish or other institution and that this broader constituency should be involved in the liturgy. Finally, ordination is an *act of the church* in a particular diocese, and that church should be gathered in the largest numbers possible for the event. Traditionally we speak of ordination "in the face of the church" — there are no private ordinations. For these reasons it is recommended that whenever possible, ordinands receive their orders in collegial groups, at the cathedral or other principal churches of the diocese, at a liturgy presided over by the diocesan bishop. This has been the norm throughout Christian history and in all prayer books until 1979, which is largely silent on the subject, perhaps reflecting the individualist culture of the 1960s and 1970s.[1] The rite's additional directions (pp. 553, ff.) give specific directions for ordinations of groups.

It would be very wrong to speak of the practice of cathedral ordinations as "doing them in batches," for in what I describe the attempt is to emphasize ritually, from the first moment, that ordained ministry is not a personal franchise, much less an individual's apotheosis, but imparts a trust that is to be carried out in community. Should an ordination overwhelming look or feel like a triumph for an individual or some group the individual may be said to represent, theft of church property may be said to have occurred. Certainly such emphases are appropriate as secondary themes as the church continues to learn the breadth of God's call, but they must not dominate a liturgy whose concern is never merely personal or ideological.

It is often said that neither a wedding nor a coronation should come to mind when witnessing an ordination, but both emphases are all too common. The bishop is in the position to insist on a rite that feels and looks like an act of the church, whose prayer is focused on individuals called to serve it pastorally, prophetically, and liturgically. When people from the entire diocese are gathered in this way, the liturgy may be quite full without misleading the worshiper — it is the church that is celebrating and praying.

If it is an argument of this chapter that the ordination of priests should be toned down and broadened a bit, it would be just as important to recognize that the ordination of deacons, especially those called to serve in that order as their primary vocation, should be just as festive as ordinations to the presbyterate.

---

1. Mitchell, who authoritatively represents the generation that produced it, takes the 1979 book to remedy the "defect" of collegial ordination of presbyters in particular, and believes they are to be ordained individually, so his witness must be taken seriously as representing the majority of the reformers' intent (119, f.). In my schema I rely on the actual text of the rubrics, the long theological tradition, and the importance of disciplined collegiality in today's church.

Ordinands should participate in the planning of the liturgy
by jointly choosing lessons, hymns, and other music, and by
selecting readers, presenters, oblation-bearers and other participants. Often choirs and musicians from their home or assigned
parishes work together with the cathedral musicians. Parishes
work together on the reception and ushering for the event as
well. The author's practice is to meet with the group to be ordained during the course of several months in order to facilitate
collegial bonding with the bishop and among the ordinands.
This process culminates in an ordination retreat taken as a
group.

Diocesan clergy know that their presence is expected at these
twice-a-year events; their presence in large numbers increases the
ordinands' experience of being grafted into a college.

It is important that the bishop preach at most if not all of these
ordinations. This is the bishop's opportunity to teach about the
nature of the church and the relationship between its clergy and
its overall life and mission.

There is occasionally some sensitivity about which non-
Anglican clergy may participate in the imposition of hands at
ordinations to the presbyterate. The perhaps obvious answer
is that those may be invited who are in communion with this
church and accept the authority of its bishops. Not infrequently
a request comes to include in the hand-laying ministers of protestant churches not in communion with this one, clergy whose
own orders were not conferred by a bishop and who do not
consider themselves under any obligation to any other order of
ministry — or to anybody at all in a few cases. The answer has
to be in the negative, not in the sense of triumphalism or supe-
riority but as a time for the healthy observance of boundaries.
To participate in the laying-on of hands is sign of collegiality
with the bishop under whose authority the new priest serves.
Ministers not episcopally ordained who join in the ordination
must be seen to do so as if acting in their own right. Thus it
is an offense against the principles of those protestant ministers
as well as against the theological understanding of orders held

by this church to include non-episcopally ordained clergy in this way. This is not a matter of saying that a member of the clergy of another community is or is not "real." It does acknowledge that our several traditions have come to hard-won understandings that are incompatible, all traditions doing the best they can with the same bank of scriptural and traditional data. We do not all understand ordained ministry in the same way, and we must be prepared to live with the uncomfortable moments that having a definite theology sometimes implies.

Many readers will be aware that Roman bishops wear the mitre for the imposition of hands at ordination. I admit that the significatory power of such a use is potent, but the practice would not work well in our setting, where hands are laid on in the middle of a solemn prayer, a circumstance in which it is the prevailing custom to bare the head. In the Roman rite, hands are laid on in complete silence, entirely outside the great prayer of ordination, so it would not seem that adopting Roman usage would be appropriate in our setting.

When necessity compels the ordination of a single individual, the practicalities discussed below can be adapted for scale. Also included in what follows is a somewhat homemade provision for publicly receiving the orders of those ordained by bishops in the historic succession who are not in communion with the Episcopal Church. This is not a common occurrence in the ordination setting, but it seemed good to share what it has looked like when it occurred. It is based on the rubrics of *The Book of Occasional Services* (pp. 237, ff.), relying on the permission given there for free adaptation. Reception of "clergy" means reception of Roman Catholics in most instances. We do not provide much public affirmation and celebration of such persons, many of whom come with a certain hesitation about their move and often have little support from family and former friends. In what follows the reader can see one attempt to fill the gap, however awkwardly.

Practicalities

At an ordination of priests the bishop will need at least two assistants, as there is a great deal for the bishop to do. For the sake of convenience, I label them Deacon1 and Deacon2 in what follows, although other persons may fulfill all those duties. Similarly, the parts I customarily assign to the archdeacon could be given to others. Additionally two or three masters of ceremonies keep the procession moving and move ordinands and other participants with fluidity and grace.

Items Needed

In the chancel

- The altar book (or authorized supplemental texts)
- prayer book and hymnal at the bishop's place
- the lectionary at the reading desk
- vessels for the eucharist, together with sufficient linens
- a chair, which the prayer book requires be in a place where all can see and hear; a faldstool works nicely. It should be placed as close to the people as possible, leaving room for the ordinands and the priests who will gather for the imposition of hands. In most of our cathedrals this in practice means somewhere near the entrance to the choir.
- cushion before the chair; the bishop will kneel on it during the litany, and the ordinands will use it later for the imposition of hands and vesting
- cushions for the ordinands to occupy during the consecration prayer before being brought forward individually for the laying-on of hands
- if used: chrism, solvent, and towels; another towel (or gremial or amice) may be used to protect the bishop's lap
- copies of the oath of conformity, or book containing them

- Bibles for the ordinands

- ordination certificates

At some convenient place

- vestments for the ordinands

- if chrism is being used, a station for the cleaning of their hands

- if desired, wine in a chalice and bread on a paten for each ordinand

- the rest of the bread, wine, and water for the celebration

The scenario assumes a rehearsal before the event. It is good for those being ordained to meet with the bishop an additional hour before the rehearsal for a time of prayer and quiet conversation, so that all enter the event in as centered a state as possible.

All presenters, bearers of gifts and tokens of ministry, and all other liturgical personnel (except clergy whose participation is restricted to the procession and laying-on of hands) must be present at the rehearsal. Exceptions to such a rule are usually fatal.

Immediately before or after the rehearsal, vestments or vessels requiring blessing are blessed by the bishop according to the forms in *The Book of Occasional Services* for vessels and that on page 552 of the prayer book in the case of vestments. (The blessing of chalices and patens is customarily, but not necessarily, reserved to the bishop.)

The rehearsal needs to begin and end promptly so that musicians can take their place and that worshipers can enter a quiet church for their own preparation.

Ordinands should be instructed to appear in a plain alb (with amice and cincture if desired). Because ordination is entrance into a college, it is well that all the albs be free of lace or apparels, or anything else likely to make an individual stand out from the group of peers. No jewelry is to be worn over the alb, and the hands are to be free of bracelets, watches, chains, and rings (except for bands given in troth). Ordinands should be advised to look "empty" so that the rite can fill. Persons with pierced ears should wear the most modest adornment or none at all.

The order of procession:

[thurifer and boat]

cross

torches

[choir]

liturgical assistants

lay members, Commission on Ministry

lay Members, Standing Committee

ordinands with their presenters

visiting clergy who will not participate in the laying-on of hands

deacons

priests of or in communion with this church

priests of the diocese

deacon with gospel book

priests who will be at the altar[2]

[canon to the ordinary]

[archdeacon]

the bishop's chaplain

[two deacons]

bishop, with staff and mitre

[two deacons]

---

2. There should be few, if any, of these, as the newly ordained take a special place with the bishop at the altar on this occasion. My own practice is to limit concelebrants to the archdeacon and canon to the ordinary, and include them only when space permits.

Experienced masters of ceremonies are vital to smooth movement into and out of the church. Sometimes sheer numbers require that the procession be broken down into smaller groups or have significant breaks so that people can conveniently take their places. In some places separate processions are formed with their own crosses, torches, and banners. Where this seems necessary, it might be better to have secondary processions led by banners than by more crosses and torches.

When all are in their places, usually at the entrance to the choir, the bishop and party reverence the altar. The altar may be censed. Facing the altar, deacon1 is to the bishop's right and deacon2 to the bishop's left. The bishop turns and hands the staff to deacon1 and the mitre to deacon2. If the altar will not be censed until the offertory, the thurible is taken out. If the altar is not to be censed, the bishop and party reverence the altar from before the faldstool. The bishop then faces the people. Deacon1 and deacon2 stand just behind the bishop's shoulders. The archdeacon stands on the cantoris or "gospel" side, facing the bishop.

Deacon1 holds the book for the bishop through the collect for purity.

The people standing, the bishop says the opening acclamation and collect for purity. After the people's Amen, the bishop sits and receives the mitre. The two deacons face the people from behind the bishop's shoulders. The archdeacon brings each ordinand with presenters before the bishop and starts the words of presentation.

Each ordinand/presenter group then steps aside until all are presented according to the formula given in the prayer book. Then the priest to be received may be presented with the words: "Bishop N., we present to you N.N., already ordained priest by a bishop in the historic succession, to be received among the clergy of this communion."[3]

---

3. When a priest is received outside of a diocesan service of this kind, this presentation should follow the creed and prayers and form the opening of the entire reception rite as outlined below.

All of those presented and their presenters stand in front of the bishop, who inquires (p. 526) about canonical requirements. The oath of conformity is signed by each of those presented and brought by the archdeacon for the bishop's counter-signature.

All stand and the bishop then inquires about the people's support for those to be ordained. The bishop removes the mitre and calls the people to prayer. Presenters return to their places, as does the priest to be received. Masters of ceremonies, and others, if necessary, lead the ordinands to places in the nave where they will prostrate themselves (or kneel) during the litany. The life-and-death, or at least intensely liminal, experience of prostration commends the practice. The masters of ceremonies assist the candidates to kneel on both knees and then to sink into the fully prone position, hands under the forehead. All others in the church kneel. At the conclusion of the litany, the bishop stands and offers the collect, one of the most ancient in the prayer book.

The bishop then sits and puts on the mitre. The dynamics of the space and occasion may suggest that the bishop put on the mitre, take the staff, and go back to the cathedra or other regular place of presidency for the liturgy of the word.

At the same time, the ordinands are assisted up from prostration by the masters of ceremonies and other assistants and conducted to their seats. Other liturgical ministers go to their seats as well.

A verger or master of ceremonies escorts a reader to the lectern.

Inasmuch as the reader is not likely to be familiar with the room and its acoustics, it is essential that readers participate in the rehearsal. Only after music has begun following the silence after "Thanks be to God" at the conclusion of the lesson is the reader escorted back to the nave.

Near the end of the first psalm or other intervenient music, the second reader is escorted to the lectern. That reader is also returned only after the silence ends at the conclusion of the lesson.

The gradual hymn or other music begins. As soon as the hymn begins, the thurifer and boat-bearer are brought to the bishop, who charges the thurible and blesses the incense. With equal dispatch, the gospel procession (which usually does not have a cross) forms. While it is forming, the deacon who is to read the gospel is brought to the bishop, asks for and receives the blessing. The bishop stands, gives the mitre to deacon2, and receives the staff from deacon1.

After announcing the gospel, the deacon censes the book left, center, and right, and hands the thurible back to the thurifer.

As the procession is returning, the bishop, who is on the way to the pulpit, meets it in time to venerate the book and goes on to preach the sermon.

When the sermon is ended, the organ and choir begin the creed, if it is sung. After the creed the bishop goes from the pulpit to the faldstool. Deacon2 and deacon1 bring mitre and staff. The bishop takes the mitre and is seated. The staff is held behind the bishop by deacon1.

All are seated except the ordinands, who stand before the bishop; the examination follows. The practice of having a representative of the ordinands kneel directly at the bishop's knees for the examination, with folded hands high on the bishop's lap (the solemn oath of Genesis 24:2, f.) should be allowed to lapse as it cannot easily speak to our culture and nowadays ordinands and bishop may be either male or female.

At the consecration of the priests, the bishop hands the mitre to deacon2. All are standing except the ordinands, who kneel facing the bishop in the order that hands will be laid on them. Presbyters are gathered to the right and left of the bishop. A master of ceremonies stands to the right of the candidate who will be the first to be ordained.

As the presbyters are coming forward, the thurifer steps out to light new coals.

The bishop removes the mitre and stands. The hymn to the Holy Spirit is sung. An acolyte holds the book to the bishop's left.

It cannot be sufficiently emphasized that our baptismal ecclesiology demands that the period of silent prayer by all of the faithful that follows the hymn be lengthy. It is useful to explain this in advance.

The bishop, still without the mitre, and with hands extended, says the prayer of consecration as deliberately and distinctly as possible.

When the bishop pauses, a master of ceremonies brings forward the first ordinand. The bishop lays on hands and the presbyters close ranks around the ordinand and add their hands — all of them need not be in direct contact with the ordinand's head. The bishop says the petition for the ordination of that individual. The bishop then pauses a beat, and only then lifts her own hands, the signal for the presbyters to remove their hands and open up the circle so that the ordinand can be led back and the next candidate brought up. This is repeated until hands have been laid on all.

Then the bishop, hands again extended, completes the prayer. The people respond with an appropriately thunderous Amen. When that Amen has finished reverberating, the new priests remain in their places, still kneeling, while those presbyters who have laid on hands return to their seats.

Tokens of Office

Music may be played or sung as the priests are vested and given the Bible and "other tokens of office" (p. 553). What follows here describes a very full expression of those gestures and tokens, from which it is easy to subtract items not desired. Traditional western texts have been modified in the direction of the liturgy and doctrine of this church. I will not argue for such practices except to point out that they are available and can explicate the trust and responsibility that ordination bestows.

These actions take place for each new priest individually as soon as possible once the music starts. The presenters line up in the aisle on the chapel side, with the vestments or instruments they present. The archdeacon stands at the right hand of deacon2. An acolyte comes to the archdeacon's side.

A presenter or presenters bring the stole and chasuble. The new priest kneels before the bishop. The bishop presents the stole to be kissed and places it on the shoulders of the new priest. The presenter and the archdeacon vest the priest in the chasuble. The new priest remains kneeling.

The bishop then gives a Bible to the newly ordained in this way: the bishop holds the Bible out at the top and the priest holds it by the bottom as the bishop says "Receive this Bible as a sign of the authority given you to preach the Word of God and to administer his holy Sacraments. Do not forget the trust committed to you as a priest of the Church of God." The archdeacon then takes back the Bible so that the new priest's hands are free for what follows.

A towel (or gremial or amice) is spread on the bishop's lap. The ordinand holds both hands out, open, touching. The bishop anoints them crosswise and then completely, saying, "The Father anointed our Lord Jesus Christ through the power of the Holy Spirit. May Jesus preserve you to sanctify the Christian people and to offer sacrifice to God." The new priest responds, "Amen." The priest's hands are not wrapped, and will shortly be cleaned.

Lay persons bring wine in a chalice and bread on a paten to the bishop. The bishop, without using the oily thumb,[4] holds them out to the new priest, who grasps them in much the same way that the Bible was taken. The bishop says, "Receive the gifts of Christ's people to be offered to God. Know what you are doing, and imitate the mystery at which you preside: model your life on the mystery of the Lord's cross."[5] *It is important to note that it is the bread and wine, not the chalice and paten* that are being given here, because the new priest is entrusted with handling what the assembly offers God in the eucharist.[6] The handing of empty

---

4. Hold the chalice by the knop with the fingers of the right hand, and the paten with the left hand.

5. I have taken significant liberties with this text on grounds of both language and theology.

6. In an atypical slip, Galley (*The Ceremonies of the Eucharist*, 226) has the empty paten and chalice given, with a form of words whose origin I cannot locate.

chalice and paten was the way of ordaining a subdeacon, who was in charge of doing the liturgical dishes. The office of subdeacon is unknown in Anglican ordinals and has been suppressed in the Roman Church.

The archdeacon takes the paten of bread and chalice of wine and gives them to an acolyte, who takes them to the credence.

As these actions are completed for each priest, she or he takes a place with the others in a chapel or other place, where a master of ceremonies or other minister assists with the cleaning of hands. All new priests return to a place near where they previously knelt.

The bishop's hands are cleaned.

The music concludes.

The Reception of the Priest

The priest whose orders are received now stands before the bishop, who says,[7]

> N., the ministry we share is none other than the sacrificial ministry of Christ, who gave himself up to death on the cross for the salvation of the world. By his glorious resurrection he has opened for us the way of everlasting life. By the gift of the Holy Spirit he shares with the Church the riches of his grace.
>
> Priests are called to proclaim his death and resurrection, to administer the Sacraments of the New Covenant that

---

7. The text that follows is from the renewal of ordination vows in The Book of Occasional Services, with a final paragraph added. *The Book of Occasional Services* permits the adaptation of the text; one adaptation I have made is the excision of the last line of *The Book of Occasional Services* rite, which is more suitable to the "Chrism Mass"; the other is moving the suggested oath of conformity to the place in the liturgy where the candidates for ordination make it. If a priest were being received outside of the context of ordination, it would be well to do the entire reception at one liturgical moment, starting with presentation and oath of conformity.

he sealed with his blood on the cross, and to care for his people in the power of the Spirit. Do you here, in the presence of Christ and his Church, renew your commitment to this ministry, under the pastoral direction of your bishop?

Answer   I do.

Bishop   Do you reaffirm your promise to give yourself to prayer and study?

Answer   I do.

Bishop   Do you reaffirm your promise so to minister the Word of God and the Sacraments of the New Covenant that the reconciling love of Christ may be known and received?

Answer   I do.

Bishop   Do you reaffirm your promise to be a faithful servant of all those committed to your care, patterning your life in accordance with the teachings of Christ, so that you may be a wholesome example to your people?

Answer   I do.

The Bishop takes the priest's right hand.

Upon these your promises, N., I admit you to the exercise of the office of priest in this Church, recognizing your authority to preach the word of God and to celebrate the Holy Mysteries with God's people. God the Father, Son and Holy Spirit bless us all through your ministry.

All answer in a loud voice   Amen.

The newly ordained and received priests now face the congregation. They are welcomed with applause. While the applause goes on, the bishop greets each of them with word and embrace before the peace (p. 534), and then offers peace to the entire assembly. The presbyters present greet the newly ordained; who then greet family members and others. The clergy and people greet one another.

The faldstool and other equipment peculiar to the ordination rite are removed from the entrance of the choir.

After an appropriate opportunity for greeting people, the new priests are conducted by the masters of ceremonies into their places in the sanctuary.

The cathedral dean or person appointed customarily offers greetings and makes necessary announcements. The bishop says the offertory sentence if there is to be one.

The liturgy continues with the offertory. Deacons prepare the table with the assistance of the MCs and others. When deacons are ordained they do this under the supervision of senior deacons in the diocese.

The bishop goes to the center of the altar, and with the assistance of the deacon, presents the gifts. The thurifer and boat-bearer appear at the altar step on the credence side. The bishop charges the thurible and blesses the incense. The bishop then censes the gifts and the altar. The deacon censes the bishop, and the rest of the incensations follow in the usual way. The bishop and other priests at the altar wash their hands.

The bishop stands at the center of the altar, surrounded by the new priests, with deacons behind each shoulder. The deacon on the left turns pages and the deacon on the right elevates the cup.

The following annotated copy of Eucharistic Prayer A is duplicated and given to candidates for practice prior to the ordination.[8] *Note:* These pages are available for download online at *www.churchpublishing.org/thebishopiscoming*

---

8. This is essentially the order laid out in Chapter Three, a little expanded and arranged for easy photocopying with enlargement.

SIDE ONE

[a clear diagram of where people will stand, then these instructions:]

Keep your hands joined before your breast through the Sanctus.

Bow profoundly with the bishop through the words "full of your glory."

Assume the orans position.

Holy and gracious Father: In your infinite love...

On the night he was handed over to suffering and death, our Lord Jesus Christ took bread;

Left hand on your breast, right hand extended toward the bread, palm up.

And when he had given thanks to you, he broke it, and gave it to his disciples, and said, "Take, eat: This is my Body, which is given for you. Do this for the remembrance of me."

The bishop will pause briefly. Rejoin your hands.

After supper he took the cup of wine;

Left hand on your breast, right hand extended toward the cup, palm up.

And when he had given thanks, he gave it to them, and said, "Drink this, all of you: This is my Blood of the new Covenant, which is shed for you and for many for the forgiveness of sins. Whenever you drink it, do this for the remembrance of me."

Rejoin your hands and immediately resume the orans position with the bishop.

SIDE TWO

Therefore we proclaim the mystery of faith...

Remain in the orans position, even though the bishop will be doing other things during the anamnesis and oblation.

We celebrate the memorial of our redemption, O Father, in this sacrifice of praise and thanksgiving. Recalling his death, resurrection, and ascension, we offer you these gifts.

Left hand on your breast, right hand out, palm down.

Sanctify them by your Holy Spirit to be for your people the Body and Blood of your Son, the holy food and drink of new and unending life in him.

As the bishop crosses herself, do so as well.

Sanctify (+) us also that we may faithfully

Rejoin your hands and immediately resume the orans position.

receive this holy Sacrament, and serve you in unity, constancy, and peace; and at the last day bring us with all your saints into the joy of your eternal kingdom. All this we ask through your Son

Jesus Christ. By him ...

Rejoin your hands before your breast through the great Amen.

After the Amen, bow profoundly with the bishop.

All assume the orans position for the Lord's Prayer.

(These sheets are for practice only and are not brought to the altar.)

The bishop breaks the bread. Silence is kept.

As the fraction anthem is sung, the new priests complete the breaking of the bread, and with the assistance of the deacons, prepare the vessels for the distribution.

The bishop says the invitation to communion. The bishop receives the sacrament and then passes a paten and then a cup in each direction for the new priests, who communicate themselves.

The new priests and others join the bishop in the distribution of Holy Communion.

After the distribution of the sacrament, the deacons and others tend the vessels.

The bishop returns to the altar.

Silence continues. Then the bishop leads the post-communion prayer.

The bishop receives the mitre and staff and blesses the people.

A deacon dismisses the assembly.

In places where the practice is observed, new priests may remain in the chancel to impart blessings. After the blessings, if any,
there are organized photography opportunities.

Ordination of Deacons

When deacons are ordained the rite is less complex because the
bishop alone imposes hands, there are fewer tokens of office, and
the new deacons do not join in the consecration of the gifts. Nonetheless, the music and other ceremonial should be of the same
richness as ordinations to the presbyterate. If a sung liturgy with
incense is the diocesan practice for ordaining priests, that should
be the practice for ordaining deacons.

New deacons share in the preparation of the table, the elevation of the chalice at the conclusion of the great thanksgiving, the
preparation of vessels, the distribution of Holy Communion, the
clearing of the table, and the dismissal. An experienced deacon
should be present at the setting and clearing of the table.

Some dioceses have a matching dalmatics for the vesting of
new deacons.

Everything should be done in a way that underscores the
integrity and dignity of the office of deacon. The sermon in particular can underscore the servanthood common to Christians,
and the distinct ministry of deacons in the church's apprehension
of and organization for effective servanthood. Even though the
churches of east and west are solidly wed to sequential ordination at least for the time being, and the majority of deacons will
become priests, the diaconate ought not ever be spoken of as a
stepping-stone to the presbyterate, just as it is impossible to imagine a sermon speaking of the presbyterate as stepping-stone to the
episcopate.

CHAPTER FIVE

Vows and Oils:
Redefining the "Chrism Mass"
with a Note on Restoration to the Ministry

General Note

The reaffirmation of ordination vows and the blessing of the oils to be used in the parishes and chaplaincies of the diocese can be a celebration for the entire diocesan community, an island of communal contact in the sometimes-lonely sea of Lent. In the author's diocese, the change from the conventional clergy-only "chrism mass" to a fully public event was received over a decade ago with enthusiasm, and lay people do come from all fourteen counties, far outnumbering the clergy present. Lunch is always provided.

The public invitation has two thrusts. In general, the diocesan community is invited to come to support their clergy. In particular, those people who have ministries of healing or catechesis, as well as those who receive these ministries, are encouraged to be present for the blessing of oils associated with the ministries. Making the liturgy emphatically public reinforces the understanding on everyone's part that ordained ministry exists in and for the church, and that everyone has a stake in the church's healing and formative ministries. It is also helpful for the clergy to sense a broad, super-parochial base of prayerful support as they attempt to serve and lead.

Experience has taught that it is best not to have this celebration on Maundy Thursday. During Holy Week it becomes a burden rather than a gift to clergy, especially to those who must drive

for several hours to attend, and attendance is required. There are
theoretical reasons to move the day as well: it is not the teaching of our formularies that the Last Supper was an ordination
liturgy, nor does our ordinal see the defining characteristic of the
presbyterate to be a personal power to confect the eucharist. Additionally, because among us deacons are always included in the
renewal of vows, it makes sense not to gather on a day that for
some people was chiefly focused on beliefs about priestly powers.
Many clergy find it useful to have this celebration in the week
before Holy Week. We have on occasion invited bishops of the
Lutheran and Moravian Churches to participate in the liturgy
and also to bring greetings from their communities at lunch time.
If the liturgy must be held on Maundy Thursday, the propers
of that day must not be used, nor should this morning celebration anticipate the foot-washing and other rituals of the evening
liturgy.

Because the prayer book provides no liturgy for such an om-
nibus public occasion, constructing this liturgy is a matter of
gathering resources and then editing them. It is thus a "Rite III"
event and accordingly leaves considerable space for adaptation
and experiment. The core of the reaffirmation of vows is that
of *The Book of Occasional Services,* to which I have added a
sentence giving the laity the punchline. The prayer book and *Enriching Our Worship 2* each provide a text for blessing the oil of
the sick and *The Book of Occasional Services* provides a fuller
blessing rite for chrism than that provided in the prayer book. Because an increasing number of our parishes in fact use the oil of
catechumens in their growing emphasis on evangelism, a prayer
had to be borrowed for that blessing. In blessing all of the oils
some bishops use sets of prayers from other sources, either traditional Anglo-Catholic or modern Roman. This seems to be within
their purview because, again, our liturgical tradition does not provide an entire rite for or in fact imagine the public diocesan event
we are considering. Nonetheless, the prayer book, *The Book of
Occasional Services,* and *Enriching Our Worship* sources seem

sufficient for most celebrations, with the addition of the prayer for oil of the catechumens.

The clergy of the diocese (including retirees and those licensed to officiate) vest, process, and sit together. Lay people associated with healing and teaching ministries read the lessons. A choir may be made up of singers from throughout the diocese. Those preparing for ordination often serve as acolytes and assistants.

The question of who stands with the bishop at the altar can be answered in several ways, none of them having proved entirely satisfactory. An un-Anglican message would be sent by massing the clergy of the diocese around the altar in something suggesting a large Roman-style concelebration. One possibility is to choose priests representative of various groups and regions in the diocese. Another is to have the bishop preside alone, attended only by deacons. In some years the bishop has been joined by the archdeacon and the canon to the ordinary. When Moravian or Lutheran bishops are present, they are always given a place at the altar.

Preparation

In addition to the equipment and books needed for any episcopal celebration, this service requires

In the nave

- oils for oil of the sick, oil of the catechumens, and chrism, all in appropriately proportioned vessels

On or near the altar

- balsam or other perfume for the chrism
- a glass wand for stirring the chrism

In the sight of all

- the faldstool set up in a place where the clergy may gather before it. *The Book of Occasional Services* (p. 238) directs that this be "before the altar," but exact proximity will be determined by visual and acoustical practicalities.

In a sacristy or workroom

– small bottles, labeled, for the oils, and equipment needed to dispense the oils. Disposable syringes have proven the easiest way to fill many bottles before the clergy have finished lunch, although a number of pumps have been devised.

The order of procession is that for episcopal liturgies, with those deacons not attending the bishop entering before the presbyters. Retired, suffragan, or assisting bishops, as well as bishops visiting from other communions, would precede the diocesan.

The propers are at the discretion of the bishop (*The Book of Occasional Services*, p. 237, suggests two possible sets that may be used effectively). The collect suggested by *The Book of Occasional Services* works well no matter what lessons are chosen. The lessons suggested in *The Book of Occasional Services* may be replaced given the circumstances and emphases current in the life of the diocese. It is sometimes helpful for lessons and sermons to emphasize healing ministry or Christian initiation, giving a bit more weight to the role of the oils in this liturgy. Sometimes the lessons are chosen to mix the themes of ministry and healing.

Because this liturgy normally occurs in Lent, its festivity is restrained. White vestments are worn, but the simple linen mitre is used. The settings of liturgical texts (Kyrie/Trisagion, creed, Sanctus, fraction anthem) are not elaborate, and perhaps not polyphonic.

The bishop vests in alb, stole, and chasuble. This is one of the occasions where bishops who sometimes wear a light dalmatic under the chasuble would do so.

The liturgy of the word proceeds as is usual at episcopal liturgies until the sermon. This is the chief occasion when this writer follows the tradition of preaching while seated, mitred, in the midst of the clergy. However, he is not able to preach and manage the staff at the same time, nor has he seen it done gracefully. The sermon can usefully celebrate the totality of the church's ministries as represented in the oils and the gathering itself. No apology should be made for taking one moment in the year ritually to support the clergy. Rather, the lay people present might well be directly thanked for their presence, knowing that their presence is appreciated as a theological act as well as a courtesy.

The Book of Occasional Services places the reaffirmation rite after the creed (sung, if possible), leaving the Prayers of the People as an option that may be included after the peace, if at all. Such a placement or omission seems to this writer quite unnatural and disruptive of our usual liturgical arc, where the peace is the bridge between liturgies of word and table, acting as both climax and gateway. Furthermore, since the rite we describe here assumes a gathered diocese, that gathering ought to pray. Since in *The Book of Occasional Services* the prayers are entirely optional and a full assembly not contemplated, in this Rite III situation prayers are appropriately offered in their normal place following the profession of faith. Finally, the peace is the usual capstone on special observance in our liturgy, and ought to follow the reaffirmation directly.

Following the prayers, for which Form V, sung, seems especially appropriate, the bishop is seated and receives the mitre. An assistant stands to the bishop's left, holding the staff. The clergy gather before the bishop. Those clergy who have come late and are seated in the nave in street clothes may need to be especially invited to join their colleagues.

The Book of Occasional Services rubrics do not contemplate the presence of lay people and therefore do not suggest a posture for them. Inasmuch as their presence is important and they are given the last word in the rite as adapted here, it is well at this point that they stand, too.

At the conclusion of the rite, *The Book of Occasional Services* has the bishop and clergy say together, "May the Lord who has given us the will to do these things, also give us the grace and power to perform them." In the writer's diocese, following this sentence, the lay people (alone) say, "May the Lord who has given you the will to do these things, also give you the grace and power to perform them, for the life of Christ's Body the Church, and for the glory of God the Holy Trinity." This little embolism, besides giving the assembly the last word, stresses what ordained ministry is for, the sustenance of the Body and the glorification of God by all the redeemed.

The peace is shared. The bishop should be careful to greet lay people, deacons, and priests. The faldstool is removed during the peace.

During the offertory lay people bring forward the eucharistic elements and the oils to be blessed. The oil for chrism will not come into play until much later, so it is placed on the presider's far left, when the presider is in the position of presidency (facing either reredos or people). The oils for the sick and catechumens are placed next to the corporal to the presider's right. If the presider for some reason were to have the altar book on the right, both of these positions for oils would be reversed. Ordinarily, extra items and stray books are not placed on the altar, so the presence of the oils there on this one occasion is a striking symbol.

The bishop censes the gifts and the altar and gives the thurible to the deacon or assisting priest for the rest of the incensations. The bishop's hands are washed here or after the blessing of the oils.

The bishop remains without mitre for the blessing of the oils. The bishop might say "let us pray for the blessing of the oil of the sick (or catechumens) before the prayer. The text for the oil of the sick is that of the prayer book (p. 455) or *Enriching Our Worship 2* (p. 37). As the initiation of adults becomes more common, programs of catechesis will expand, and the anointing of catechumens will likely increase as the church takes greater corporate responsibility for their formation. A text for the blessing of the oil for the catechumens might follow this (slightly modified) Roman prayer.

Holy God, protector of all who believe in you, bless this oil and give wisdom and strength to all who are anointed with it in preparation for their baptism. Bring them to a deeper understanding of the gospel, and lead them to the joy of new birth, through Jesus Christ our Lord.

The vessels of oil for the sick and for catechumens are removed to credence or sacristy. Those who are joining the bishop at the altar now approach, and the great thanksgiving begins.

The post-communion prayer may be either one of those on pp. 365–66 or that for ordinations (inserting "we pray that all who are ordained to serve your church" for the ordinand's name).

The ingredients for the chrism are brought to the center of the altar, before the bishop. Without the mitre the bishop addresses the people (*The Book of Occasional Services* p. 235), either in the words provided or "similar words." The writer has alternated between *The Book of Occasional Services* text and "similar" but more visually rich words from other rites.[1] The fragrance is then mixed into the oil with the wand. There is a tradition of the bishop breathing into the vessel (and, formerly, saying "Ruach," the Hebrew for "spirit"), but no modern rite demands the practice. The bishop places a hand on the vessel and says the prayer of blessing.

After the people's Amen, the vessels are removed. In Lent the bishop then says the Prayer Over the People (*The Book of Occasional Services* pp. 25, 26). Otherwise the bishop gives a blessing and the dismissal follows.

Restoration to Ministry

There are instances where those who have been deprived of the exercise of their ministry for any of a number of reasons are to be

---

1. The Bishop of Alaska reports that when native people first encountered the 1979 prayer book they had no doctrinal concerns but observed of its language that "there are no pictures in it."

restored. *The Book of Occasional Services* (p. 237) rite for reaffirmation of vows is the core of the restoration observance. Beyond
the modest directions *The Book of Occasional Services* provides,
it is suggested that normally restoration would not be articu-
lated liturgically in a large gathering, but that the bishop and
the person to be restored would make a decision that respects the
position of all who may have been affected by the circumstances
that led to the deposition, resignation, or long-term suspension.
The balance to be struck is between the pastoral necessities that
the reaffirmation be public and the restoration emotionally real,
and the pastoral necessity to distinguish between restoration and
vindication.

The liturgy follows the normal pattern for an episcopal celebration, except that the faldstool or chair is placed where it is situated
when orders are conferred. After the prayers of the people, which
may be crafted as litanies for ministry, the church, or its mission, the bishop puts on the mitre and goes to the faldstool. An
assistant holds the staff to the bishop's left. The priest or deacon to be restored, perhaps accompanied by the president of the
Standing Committee, archdeacon, or other supporter, stands before the bishop. There is no presentation. According to the rubric
(*The Book of Occasional Services,* p. 240) the priest or deacon
appears without stole, chasuble, or dalmatic. The rite of reaffirmation (*The Book of Occasional Services,* p. 238) follows with
some changes. As per the rubric, the oath of conformity is inserted
as the last question. Inasmuch as the rubric gives permission to
adapt this rite for reception and restoration, it is suggested that
following the oath of conformity, the bishop stand, take the staff,
and make some short declaration of the restoration. Such adaptation might in some circumstances also include the excision of
the two short passages beginning, "And now ... " and "May the
Lord ... ," the rite proceeding directly the "personal greeting"
(*Book of Occasional Services,* p. 240) of the restored priest or
deacon — it seems that a sincere embrace here would be much
more powerful than an exchange of words and on some occasions
may effectively teach Luke 15:20. Even if the text is not adapted,

the personal greeting rubric should be given full observance. After the peace the newly-restored priest or deacon assumes the stole (and other vestments) and takes an appropriate presbyteral or diaconal role in the celebration of the eucharist. It is assumed that *The Book of Occasional Services* places the vesting after the peace so as not to appear to mimic the ordination rite.

CHAPTER SIX

Solemn Evensong

At diocesan conventions and on feast days the bishop will often preside at fully choral evensong with incense. A liturgy that is sung and where incense is employed is called "solemn," hence the expression Solemn Evensong.

When the choir alone sings the psalms, canticles, and litany, the bishop and people always sit, stand, or kneel as usual for those parts of the service. Service settings of such elaborateness that the appropriate postures of worship seem ludicrous are best not employed in the worship of, for instance, a diocesan convention, where many members of the assembly may not be familiar with a contemplative approach to liturgical music.

The bishop vests in alb, stole, and cope, with cross, mitre, and staff. Some writers prefer to omit the stole. Deacons assisting the bishop wear (stole and) dalmatic. The entrance follows the pattern normal for episcopal liturgies, except that after handing off the mitre and staff, the bishop venerates the altar with a bow alone. Whether or not the candle-lighting ceremony is observed, the bishop begins the office at the chair, and resumes the mitre and sits for the psalms.

The principle of proportionality among elements of the rite that has controlled other recommendations in this book suggests that better balance in the liturgy is maintained by censing the altar during the Magnificat rather than earlier at the Phos Hilaron. After the first lesson, as the Magnificat is being introduced, the thurible is brought to the bishop's chair, where it is charged by the bishop. The bishop and all stand. The bishop, without the mitre, is led to the altar by the thurible bearer and any other necessary assistants.[1] The altar is venerated with a bow alone. The bishop censes the altar and cross. Then the bishop and all others present are censed by the deacon or other assistant.

The bishop returns to the chair and resumes the mitre. The second lesson is read without any of the ceremonial attendant upon the gospel at the eucharist, and its canticle is sung, all standing. The mitre is removed for the Apostles Creed and prayers, and resumed for the blessing.

On occasions when another officiant sings the office when the bishop is present in the chair, the bishop may cense the altar and say the prayers after the anthem, and always gives the blessing.

When the bishop is present at simpler celebrations of the office, choir dress (with scarf and hood, if desired) is appropriate, and the bishop may say prayers after the anthem and always gives the blessing.

---

1. Modern copes rarely need to be held open for the wearer because of weight or dimensions, but in some cases involving antique vestments this remains a necessity.

CHAPTER SEVEN

Institutions, Weddings, and Funerals

Institution of Ministers

We now call this rite "Celebration of a New Ministry," and it can be adapted for use other than the institution of rectors. It can be used for instituting priests into a variety of offices, and for installing lay persons and deacons, although its most common use is for rectors and vicars. Consequently I shall refer consistently to rectors, knowing that the reader will make any needed adjustments for the limitless variations possible. Elaborate liturgies for installing clergy are a relatively recent development in Anglican liturgy. Before the advent of these liturgies, 1804–08 in the Episcopal Church, the custom was for the new incumbent to receive a letter of appointment and then to move into the rectory and the following Sunday "read himself in." That is, presiding at the liturgy established the rector or vicar's presence and place.

It is still true that this liturgy is not required. Canonical selection and a letter of institution make one a rector, for instance. The rite says that it is a gathering to "welcome" the new minister. That is what the rite sets out to do. It is a mistake to fault it for being what it intends to be. It is not a mistake to question the scope of those intentions, however, and it is widely believed that the rite will be replaced entirely or that alternatives will be soon provided.

As far as it goes, the intention to welcome is perfectly legitimate and pastorally helpful. There will be few enough moments of encouragement and support as years pass, so beginning the honeymoon period with a celebration certainly seems good. There is a great deal to be said for allowing the parish to care for the new minister without having their care trumped by some act on the new minister's part. The parish has the power in this liturgy as it stands. They give.

At the same time, given the shifts in our ecclesiology, the question arises of just to *what* we are welcoming the new minister. Few parishes explicitly operate on pure hierarchical principles ("father/mother knows best"), and clergy are increasingly seen as leaders of, rather than as surrogates for, the whole team. They are seen as stewards of word and sacrament, and not as their proprietors. Consequently there is, de facto, a great deal of adjustment made within this liturgy throughout the church, and I will suggest some possibilities myself after examining the celebration of the rite as it stands. It is hoped that these suggestions will be made unnecessary as proposals may well come to the 2006 and 2009 General Conventions for revision of the institution liturgy.*

Clergy who are new to the diocese will need coaching as to the flavor of diocesan celebrations (for instance, I require that all clergy be invited to ordinations and institutions regardless of their gender or other identity). In the final chapter I have provided our customary for institutions as an example.

To keep the focus on the parish's welcome, it is best to shape the rite so that it not be mistaken for ordination. There is no prostration for the litany. Inasmuch as the litany for ordinations is not required to be used, it is best to use one of the newer litanies for the church, mission, or evangelism. Each does a good job of praying the ecclesiology into which we increasingly live. Similarly, although the prayer book allows vesting as an option, it seems better for the new minister to appear fully vested. Nothing should be done to suggest that presbyterate is conferred in this liturgy. This distinction has become more important as our contacts with the Lutherans increase for three reasons: they will

---

*The 2006 General Convention authorized trial use of a rite of "The Renewal of Ministry with the Welcoming of a New Rector" or other pastor, available electronically as *Enriching Our Worship 4* at *www.churchpublishing.org*. The trial rite raises as many questions as it answers.

in fact "de-roster" a member of the clergy who goes too long
without being installed in some definable ministry; some of their
technical theologians see ordination as merely "the first installa-
tion" in a pastor's life; and their bishops are installed rather than
ordained to a distinct order.

Invariably, when the new rector also tries to be master of
ceremonies for this liturgy, there have been moments of chaos
or exhaustion, or both. It is a service to the new minister for
the bishop to insist that there be a master of ceremonies to
carry organizational and logistical burdens during the celebration. The liturgical committee of the diocese makes available
people with skills in this ministry, so rectors new to the diocese
do not necessarily have to take chances in selecting a master of
ceremonies.

It seems good to schedule the institution earlier rather than
later in the honeymoon period, and this can mean utilizing the
provision for a person other than the bishop to preside.

The Institution. For this opening section (BCP, pp. 559, ff.) the
bishop sits, mitred, in the faldstool or other chair in a place where
all can see or hear. Ideally no extra seating would be required,
and the bishop would sit in the normal place of presidency, but
the ideal is not often the case. An assistant holds the staff to the
bishop's left. Where physical circumstances are cramped, and the
bishop has not delegated the reading of the letter of institution or
has opted not to read the letter at all, it may be workable for all
to stand during the brief introduction.

The bishop removes the mitre for the litany, and resumes it
after the collect. The bishop who uses a faldstool for the opening
rites could retire from it to the normal place of presidency for the
liturgy of the word.

The bishop preaches or designates the preacher. The sermon
can be followed by responses, including remarks by the new rector. I have found it helpful to have as such "response" the renewal
of baptismal vows, with the new rector standing with the congregation in the nave, leading their response to the questions posed
by the bishop. This use is a way to emphasize the new rector's

solidarity with the people as fellow disciple playing by the same rules and for the same end.

The Induction. The bishop is seated, with the mitre, for this section, except for the handing over of the water. There seems to be no moment in the prayer book liturgy more prone to excess than this modest provision for giving symbolic "tools of the trade" to the new rector, acts intended to express the parish's hopes for the ministry about to begin. History may well judge this provision mistake, as the *traditio instrumentorum* (handing over the tools of the trade) is associated with ordination. Priests should be encouraged to keep this modest rite modest. It is my experience that the weirder the gifts that are given (teddy bears and entrenching tools stand out in my memory) the shorter the rectorship. I ask rectors to review with me anything out of the ordinary in the Induction, and to simply remove anything cute or cloying. Rectors are to be encouraged to remain in receptive, grace-receiving mode, and not to attempt to top the people's gifts with a gift to the parish. Attempts to even the score or perhaps trump the people's generosity are counter-productive to the liturgy's intention to welcome.

If the new rector elects to say the prayer of self-dedication (p. 562), the bishop and assembly stand, and the bishop removes the mitre.

For the presentation of the rector to the congregation the bishop puts on the mitre. It is important to know beforehand if the rector's family is to be presented, and how they wish to be spoken of in the third person. After the applause the bishop greets the new minister, who then offers the peace to the entire assembly. During the peace the bishop should greet the rector's family, parish leaders, and others in proportion to time and numbers present. The new minister is the principal agent of greeting, however.

At the Eucharist. The pattern for eucharists at parish visitations is followed, the new rector in close proximity to the bishop. Together with the bishop the new rector should administer bread. The new rector pronounces the final blessing.

Alternatives. New rectors and liturgical planners of all liturgical stripes have asked if any alternative is available to the prayer book institution rite. Their common concern was the ability to have a "complete" liturgy with appropriate music and the ability to avoid what they consider the poor or clericalized ritual of the prayer book rite. As the objected-to aspects of the rite are not subject to easy adaptation, the alternative in their case seems to be not to use the Celebration of New Ministry at all: its liturgy is not required before a rector can take office. Instead there may simply be a special eucharist presided over by the bishop. After the sermon, renewal of baptismal vows (or sung creed) and prayers of the people or litany, the Letter of Institution may be read, a welcome from the wardens or other leaders offered, and the peace shared. The presentation of any gifts can take place at the reception or dinner that follows the liturgy.

Another possibility is to follow the above outline but with provision for a celebration of the eucharist where the bishop is present but does not preside at the altar (see Chapter Three).

Finally, since none of this is required, there might simply be a eucharist in the parish at which the rector preaches and presides, at which the lay people, before the peace, make statements and gestures of welcome. The Letter of Institution may be conveyed privately.

The Celebration and Blessing of a Marriage

The bishop normally presides at the weddings of clergy and candidates for ordination, and may well preside at other weddings, particularly those of the poor. The ceremonial is much the same as when a priest presides, but some differences require attention.[1]

The vestments are those for the eucharist, with cross, mitre and staff. Weddings are still occasionally celebrated without the

---

1. A bishop who has not seen the first twenty minutes of Robert Altman's 1978 film, *A Wedding,* has missed the American cinema's most pungent comment on episcopal ceremonial, among other things.

eucharist, and on those occasions the bishop vests in alb, stole, and cope, with cross, mitre, and staff.

The mitre is worn for the opening address and the consent, for the marriage (except the blessing of the rings), the final paragraph of the blessing of the marriage, the peace, and not again until blessing at the end of the eucharist. The episcopal blessing may be used.

"When both a bishop and a priest are present and officiating, the bishop should pronounce the blessing and preside at the Eucharist" (BCP, p. 422). That rubric describes a minimum, and allows for full participation by clergy who may have a special pastoral and personal relationship to those being married. Unless such personal relationships exist so as to warrant the division of presidency, it is preferable that other clergy read the gospel, perhaps preach, read the prayers, join the bishop at the altar, and assist with the distribution of Holy Communion.

It is the practice in some places for the bishop to be part of a procession at marriages. This does not seem helpful: the natural focus of ritual attention is the couple, and as in the present culture many of the assembly will not be acquainted with the uses of the church, two processions may confuse. "I didn't know my daughter was going to be married by a chess piece," remarked one slightly inebriated non-Christian father of the bride on the occasion of a grand episcopal entrance. It is best for the bishop and other clergy to enter by the shorter way, which is usually through the choir but may be directly from the sacristy. It may have been a good idea in instances like that just related to advise people at the rehearsal as to what they should expect in terms of vesture and practice in the Episcopal Church. Because the bishop seldom conducts the rehearsal, those in charge might be reminded of this.

Funerals

Except in very unusual circumstances the bishop presides at the funerals of diocesan clergy and predecessor bishops. The bishop is also often the presider at the funerals of clergy spouses and children. In addition, the bishop on occasion presides at the funerals of members of the diocese, particularly lay leaders.

Clergy and their families should be kept aware of this tradition so that they do not feel that it is an imposition to ask the bishop to preside. Rather, they should understand that it is both the duty and desire of the bishop to minister pastorally and liturgically at the time of death.

Practice saying the words. When we work with and love someone, no matter how skilled we are liturgically, there is the possibility that one will break up when it comes time to say some parts of the burial liturgy. Liturgical leadership means ministering to the assembly more than it means processing one's own emotions. To be an effective liturgical minister, one must deal with one's own grief, anger, or other emotions well before the liturgy. Often this means reading it aloud in private and letting the emotional response happen in that private moment. I find that the commendatory prayers can be quite heavy emotionally, and find that I must go through them several times before the liturgy. Similarly, actually writing out the sermon before the funeral is a way to get one's grieving done to a level sufficient to promise effective liturgical ministry. The more closely one is associated with a priest, spouse, or fellow bishop, the more important it is to do this pre-processing. Nothing is gained for the gospel by drawing attention to one's own grieving. Perhaps "Jesus wept" is the shortest verse in the Bible for a reason; there was more work to do for God's glory and the mourners in Bethany.

There was a time when the staff was not carried at funerals, reflecting a somewhat sentimental notion that the bishop had lost jurisdiction over the departed. This practice is no longer observed. The bishop is the chief pastor to all those present, and the vestments and insignia are those for any eucharist, except that the plain linen mitre is worn. If the bishop does not preside at the altar, the cope replaces the chasuble.

When an ordained person is to be buried, the coffin is arranged so that the deceased lies facing the assembly. When a lay person is buried, the coffin is arranged so that the deceased faces the altar. This venerable tradition is meant to recall the deceased's role in the liturgical assembly. The paschal candle, lit, is near the coffin. In some places it is the custom at the funeral of a cleric to place insignia of the deceased's order on the coffin, over the pall.

After the reception of the body, the procession is organized as for any episcopal celebration, and precedes the coffin. This both gives the deceased the place of honor in the procession and leaves access to the altar uncomplicated. After the post-communion prayer, the bishop walks with mitre and staff to the coffin. At the coffin, the bishop hands off the mitre and staff, leads the commendation, and herself incenses the coffin where that is the practice. The bishop resumes the mitre and staff and either blesses the people (BCP, p. 483) or waits at the chair to take part in the procession to the grave.

The blessing of the grave and committal are said without staff and mitre, which are resumed for the blessing and return to the church.

When burial is in the church the commendation is omitted and the committal service follows the post-communion prayer. If the final resting place in the church is not in sight of the entire assembly, the bishop returns to the chair or another visible place for the blessing and deacon's dismissal.

CHAPTER EIGHT

Through the Liturgical Year

It is good for the bishop to emphasize the importance of the liturgical year by arranging to be present in various places in the diocese at major observances of the year. Certainly the cathedral has a claim on the bishop's presence for principal Christmas and Easter celebrations, but other observances around those feasts along with other holy days are times to be in the diocese. One bishop attempts to be with parishes on their feasts of title; another is in different parts of the diocese for Christmas Eve and Christmas Day, the Easter Vigil and Easter Day.

Like many bishops, I have actively solicited invitations for holy days, and some parishes have a kind of claim on certain dates. For instance, I am always to be found in a particular parish on the Presentation, and in particular regions for All Saints and Corpus Christi celebrations. I try to be in different parishes in different regions for the many observances of Holy Week. Recently parishes have staked claims on the observance of the First Book of Common Prayer and New Year's Eve. These occasions are not official visitations and no business is conducted, allowing bishop and people simply to enjoy a common experience of worship.

Anciently, bishops were known to emphasize the forty days of Lent by presiding and preaching in a different church each day, and some modest approximation of that ministry is worth considering in our own age.

Ash Wednesday

The bishop wears the plain linen mitre for the address (BCP, p. 264), but removes it for the blessing of ashes, Psalm 51, and litany of penitence. Ashes are imposed on the bishop's forehead by an assisting minister. Traditionally, if the bishop imposes ashes, the mitre is worn, but our common humanity is perhaps stressed more effectively by its omission. In any case, the white mitre is in some jeopardy until all hands (and the episcopal forehead) are cleansed.

Procession with Palms on Passion Sunday

Confirmation and other initiatory rites are not celebrated on this day, but the bishop should be the visible leader of the diocese's celebration of Holy Week.

The procession with palms was originally a stand-alone liturgy, celebrated in the afternoon by the Jerusalem church. Its subsequent connection to the eucharist at which the Passion is read creates rather a lot of liturgy. Somewhat paradoxically, this can be endured only if hurry is not sensed, so while sermon and other elements of the liturgy need to be somewhat compact, they must be solid. Abbreviated passion readings and processionless palm blessings give the worshiper the impression that this day's liturgy is simply to be gotten through, its bases touched, when in fact its goal is to lead all into deeper contemplation of the mystery of redemption.

The procession begins in a space apart from the church. The bishop is vested in alb, stole, and cope or chasuble, with cross, staff, and simple mitre. The mitre is removed for the processional gospel and blessing of the branches. The bishop resumes the mitre, receives a palm branch, and an assistant carries the staff in the procession.

Once in the church, the bishop hands off the branch and mitre, and reverences the altar. If the bishop has worn a cope, it is removed and replaced with the chasuble either before reverencing the altar or at the chair after the reverence. If more than one person reads the passion, the bishop blesses all readers. Neither candles nor incense are used for the passion reading.

"Corpus Christi"

The new bishop may be, as I was, nonplussed when receiving an invitation to preside at a Corpus Christi celebration in an Anglo-catholic parish. In the path my life had followed I had not had occasion to witness such a celebration for two decades, and discovered that hurried recourse to various Anglican priest's manuals was not sufficient, as the usual ceremonial changes when a bishop presides. Consequently what follows here may be yet another survival guide, and a somewhat detailed one, because parishes who hold such celebrations have high expectations.

No contemporary western church actually has a liturgy entitled "Corpus Christi," which is a nickname. Among Anglicans, the prayer book propers "Of the Holy Eucharist" are in many places used on the Thursday after Trinity Sunday (or at some other occasion after Pentecost) for a eucharistic festival. Roman Catholics and some Lutherans refer to the liturgy using those propers as the Solemnity of the Lord's Body and Blood. The observance sometimes includes a procession with the sacrament, followed by other devotions and a blessing with the sacrament.

The liturgy is celebrated as are all episcopal eucharists, except that an additional host is placed on the paten or corporal at the offertory. The second host is not consumed during communion. At the end of the distribution of Holy Communion, the deacon places the second host in the monstrance. Parishes that have monstrances will expect the bishop and all liturgical ministers to genuflect toward the exposed sacrament. The bishop returns to the chair for the post-communion collect.

As music is played or sung, the bishop may remove the chasuble and put on a cope, but not the mitre, which along with the staff will not see further use in this liturgy.[1] Incense is placed in the thurible. The bishop kneels before the altar and incenses the sacrament with three (perhaps double) swings. Silence follows.

---

1. The Roman rite has the staff carried before the bishop in the procession with the sacrament, but this seems to distract visually from the procession.

Then a long cloth called a humeral veil (literally, a veil worn over shoulder and upper arms) is placed over the bishop, and drapes her hands. The bishop then goes to the altar, genuflects, and takes the monstrance in both veiled hands.

The procession is formed as usual, except that the thurible (some places use two thuribles) immediately precedes the bishop bearing the sacrament. In some places a canopy is carried over the sacrament, but the reader is warned that a great deal of practice is required to coordinate its use. When it is used poorly, something between slapstick and sacrilege occurs, effectively sabotaging the liturgy beyond human power to repair (sadly, I do not speak from theory alone here).

The procession goes to another church, or to an outdoor altar. If no alternative is possible, the procession returns to the altar from which it started. Upon arrival at whatever altar is to be used, the bishop stands before it. The deacon to the bishop's right takes the monstrance from the bishop and places it on the altar. The bishop and deacon genuflect and take their places before the altar, where they kneel. The humeral veil is removed from the bishop. Incense is brought. The bishop incenses the sacrament. A hymn is sung (often, *Tantum ergo Sacramentum, The Hymnal 1982*, 330).

Appropriate prayers are then said. The bishop receives the humeral veil (placed on her shoulders by assistants), stands, goes to the altar and genuflects. The bishop takes the monstrance as before, turns, and makes the sign of the cross over the people in silence.

After the blessing, the deacon takes the monstrance from the bishop and places it on the altar. The bishop and deacon genuflect. The bishop kneels in front of the altar while the deacon takes the sacrament to the place where it is reserved. When this has been done, the veil is removed from the bishop by those who had placed it on the shoulders.

If the procession has not gone to another church or chapel but to an outdoor altar at a distance from the church, the procession may need to return to the church, where the bishop and deacon will do the things just described.

The bishop and assistants then return to the sacristy without further ceremony other than customary reverences.

If there is no procession but the sacrament is to be exposed and the blessing given, the bishop need not exchange the chasuble for the cope, but the cope is in practice usually put on. Meanwhile the deacon puts the host consecrated for the purpose into the monstrance, which is placed on the center of the altar. The deacon genuflects and takes her place outside the rail. The bishop returns, kneels before the altar with all others. The sacrament is censed. The hymn and prayers follow. Silence is kept. The bishop rises, goes to the altar, genuflects, and with the humeral veil lifts the monstrance and blesses the people with the host, saying nothing.

The bishop returns the monstrance to the altar. A deacon rises and genuflects, and removes the sacrament, placing it in the aumbry. When this has been done, the bishop, clergy, and servers make the customary reverences and leave the sanctuary.

CHAPTER NINE

Specimen Customaries and Documents

Each of these specimens is very much in the writer's personal idiom and none is suggested for use as is. Rather, they are examples of how one bishop touches the bases.

Each of these specimens has several purposes. While managing practicalities, they also do a bit of catechesis. This seems important both from the point of view of continuing education as well as acceptance of the reality that clergy in our church have widely varying backgrounds in the content and use of the prayer book. They also set some boundaries while leaving room for variety and adaptation.

> NOTE: These customaries and documents are downloadable for local use and adaptation at
>
> *www.churchpublishing.org/thebishopiscoming*

Revisions will be posted on the site as appropriate. You may also contact the writer at this site.

I. Customary for Confirmation/Reception/Reaffirmation

> Note: There may be pastoral reasons to make ex-
> ceptions to the guidelines that follow. Please do not
> hesitate to discuss any such concerns with the bishop.

Before the service:

* If possible, please have the group being confirmed/received
  or making reaffirmation meet with the bishop briefly for
  introductions and a prayer at least 20 minutes *before the
  service.*

* Please be doubly sure to have rehearsed them in the parts of the
  service they are to speak, and remind them to bring their prayer
  books or service leaflets with them when they are presented.
  Their being able to participate is of the first importance.

The bishop will not second-guess you about whom you present
for confirmation and whom for reception, as situations can become very complex. The bishop explains his view, for what it
is worth, in the appendix to this customary. As long as faith
is professed and hands are imposed, it would seem that ritual
sufficiency is reached.

The color for the service is that of the season, except that white
or red may be worn on otherwise "green" days. Green remains a
perfectly acceptable color. Please advise the bishop of your choice.

Please also advise the bishop as to which parts of the service
your congregation has some experience of as sung. Where possible and not a burden, the bishop would prefer that there we sing
the dialogue ("sursum corda"), preface, doxology ("by whom
and with whom . . . ") and its great Amen, [Lord's prayer], pontifical blessing, and the dismissal. If none of this is a comfortable
possibility for your parish, please say so. Please be sure to print
the text of the pontifical blessing (in the altar book p. 232, and
The Hymnal 1982 S-173) in the service folder, even if it is not to
be sung.

Please use the propers of the day for all Sunday morning con-firmations. On other occasions we will need to discuss the choice of lessons.

The deacon or priest reading the gospel should come to the bishop for a blessing before going to the place where the gospel is read. After "The Gospel of the Lord" and the people's response, the gospel book should be brought to the bishop, open, for veneration.

Presentation and Examination of the Candidates

The bishop wishes to make eye contact with all the candidates during the examination and baptismal covenant, so they should be arranged in a semi-circle or other convenient group near the bishop's chair.

During the prayers for the candidates, unless the baptismal liturgy is being celebrated and the congregation is already on page 305 of the prayer book, do not announce the page number or indicate it in the leaflet, as a long pause to turn pages here just confuses people, and they must turn back. *It is simplest to say, "the response to the petitions is, 'Lord, hear our prayer.' "* Then just start praying without indicating a page number in the service folder or by way of announcement. Please do use this litany, and *insert any local needs or concerns* in petitions of similar form, with the same response, at the end of the petitions for the candidates. The bishop will then conclude with the collect. If you elect to use Eucharistic Prayer D, local petitions can be put there in the "remember" section, if you like; but using Prayer D in an already-lengthy rite is not the bishop's first choice. (Please keep in mind that the "remember" sections in Prayer D are addressed to God, not the congregation, and should be written accordingly.)

At the time for confirmation, reception, or reaffirmation, please bring the candidate to the bishop and pronounce his or her name distinctly. Even if candidates wear name cards, present them by name, because some names are not easy to pronounce without hearing them. If the candidates are to be received or are making a reaffirmation, indicate that as well. Candidates for all three rites kneel.

If the architecture permits the group to stay together, please do not send the candidates back to their seats. This enables the bishop to greet each one at the peace.

After the peace, please make any necessary announcements; the bishop will then say the offertory sentence.

The deacon or priest who sets the table should put the chalice and paten side by side, not front and back, with chalice on the right.

The bishop is accustomed to use the lavabo.

BCP, p. 322: "It is appropriate that the other priests present stand with the celebrant at the Altar, and join in the consecration of the gifts...." Thus, at the eucharist, priests in the parish should join the bishop. Please see the customary for celebrations at which the bishop presides for details. Reminder: lay persons should assist with the chalice only after all the clergy of the parish are fulfilling their servant ministry of feeding. The rector or priest in charge *must* join the bishop is distributing Holy Communion.

At visitations, we use either Rite I or II *according to the use your parish follows,* from the offertory on. You may select the eucharistic prayer. Prayers A and B are preferred for these occasions. If you select Prayer D, you or a deacon should read the "remember" intercessions in the places indicated.

Vessels for the distribution should be made ready during the fraction anthem, before the invitation is said. Concelebrants will communicate themselves.

The benediction is ordinarily the episcopal blessing, said or sung, as you desire. In Lent the Prayers over the People from BOS is used.

The dismissal should be said facing the people.

APPENDIX

"In the course of their Christian development, those baptized at an early age are expected, when they are ready and have been duly prepared, to make a mature public affirmation of their faith and commitment to the responsibilities of their Baptism and to receive the laying on of hands by the bishop.

"Those baptized as adults, unless baptized with laying on of hands by a bishop, are also expected to make a public affirmation of their faith and commitment to the responsibilities of their Baptism in the presence of a bishop and to receive the laying on of hands."

A *personal viewpoint*

As mentioned above, I will not second guess you about whom you present for confirmation and whom for reception. What follows is how I understand the matter. I acknowledge that there are other approaches very much alive in the church, and do not in any sense insist on my interpretation.

I take the paragraphs just quoted from the Book of Common Prayer in their plain and literal sense. In our church confirmation is understood to be a combination protestant/catholic moment when a baptized person takes an adult stand for Christ in the presence of the local church and before the bishop as representative of the catholic church, and then receives the laying-on of hands (with anointing) for strengthening by the Holy Spirit. This is not what many protestant groups intend, *regardless of how many years of instruction or depth of Bible learning the process involves.*

Thus everyone who has not yet made a "mature public affirmation of their faith and commitment to the responsibilities of their Baptism" before a bishop in the historic succession is appropriately presented for confirmation. This specifically includes Roman Catholics who received the very differently-intended Roman rite of confirmation while a child, and specifically includes the Orthodox, whose (repeatable) rite of chrismation is not equated to confirmation in their theology when they talk among themselves. The idea of chrismation being the same as confirmation was developed for the benefit of western thinkers at the Council of Florence, when the idea was introduced in order to get foreign aid for the Armenians by demonstrating that they really did have the same number of sacraments as had Rome. Similarly, the notion of chrism as a virtual "bishop in a bottle" does not bear the stamp of antiquity.

Basically, according to the literal sense of the prayer book, the only people to be presented for "reception into communion," then, are those former Roman Catholics whom you are convinced have already made a *mature* public affirmation of their faith before a bishop in historic succession. The relationship with the Lutherans complicates this tremendously, and I will trust the decision you and the candidate make, but please remember that almost no Lutheran has been confirmed by a bishop, whether in or out of historic succession. Also, when Roman Catholic adults are confirmed, it is by the priest who prepared them. My expectation is that the confusion will be dealt with in the next round of liturgical revision by returning to the proposal of the 1970s for a single rite for reaffirmation. In the meantime, my tactical solution is that both those confirmed and received receive the laying-on of hands (and chrismation). This solution is experiencing broad use, and coming to be called "reception with the laying-on of hands." Notwithstanding everything I have written, *please do not make the decision whether to present for confirmation or reception become a stumbling block for those who have scruples in the matter.*

I am happy to discuss any questions you or candidates might have.

II. Customary for the Institution of Ministers

Note: There may be unusual circumstances or pastoral reasons sufficient to make exceptions to the guidelines that follow. Please do not hesitate to discuss any such concerns with the bishop.

In response to fairly constant demand, there is an alternative to this liturgy suggested in an appendix to this customary.

In the still-developing baptismal ecclesiology of the Episcopal Church, this service has become something of a whipping-child, and there can be no question about its status as the least satisfying piece of the 1979 revision. That said, there remains something to affirm about its somewhat clerical shape, and you will have the rest of your ministry to teach and enact special emphases of your ecclesiology. This liturgy has another purpose within that baptismal ecclesiology: it is a chance for the baptized and your colleagues to welcome and ritually support you in the challenging ministry you undertake — possibly the only or last experience of organized support you will receive. Let it happen. Let yourself be cared for; it is arguable that you will teach more by gracefully receiving than by designing "statement" liturgical embolisms.

The observations below follow the rite in the prayer book, under the italicized or bold section indicators as the prayer book presents them.

A few general notes:

- Please, *do not make this service look or feel like an ordination.*

- Please do not prostrate for the litany.

- Please be fully vested as a concelebrant of the eucharist from the very beginning of the service. Any other vestments you receive can be placed with the keys, books, oil, and other items brought to you as symbolic gifts.

- It is suggested that you use a litany other than that for ordinations, particularly new litanies for the church, mission, or evangelism.

- Ordinarily, the bishop will preach at institutions. If you have special requests, please speak with the bishop directly. In any event, a guest preacher should be acquainted with the spiritual resources and mission possibilities of the parish.

- Please also note the additional directions on page 564 of the prayer book.

- The color for the service is white or red, white always being used in Eastertide. Outside of Eastertide, please advise the bishop of your choice.

- Please also let the bishop know which parts of the service your congregation has some experience of as sung (this is not the same question as whether or not you personally can sing). Where possible and not a burden or a novelty, it is preferable that we sing at least the dialogue ("sursum corda"), preface, doxology ("by whom and with whom . . . ") and its great Amen.

- Please use a master of ceremonies in this service; it really will make a difference in how you can relax and experience the worship. Members of the diocesan Commission on Liturgy and Music are at your disposal for consultation.

The Institution

The wardens may be joined by other presenters, at your option.

The archdeacon will normally be present with the bishop and will read the letter of institution.

You kneel at the entrance of the chancel or other central place during the litany. Again, prostration is not appropriate.

At the Liturgy of the Word

Please select the lessons, the lay persons to read them, and a gospel, to be read by a deacon if at all possible (a deacon almost always accompanies the bishop). If there will be deacons present, a priest should not read the gospel. Please notify the preacher as early as you can of the lesson choices.

The deacon or priest reading the gospel should come to the bishop for a blessing before going to the place where the gospel is read. After "The Gospel of the Lord" and the people's response, the gospel book, if there is one, should be brought, still open, to the bishop for veneration.

The sermon may be followed by responses, including words from you. Some find it helpful for the first response to be the renewal of baptismal vows by new rector and people, as introduction to the Induction. With rector and people answering together, solidarity in discipleship is clearly expressed, and the Induction has a more communal context.

The Induction

This modest symbolic expression of the hopes for and responsibilities of the person instituted needs to remain in proportion. You have been called here because you are a talented and caring person. Hard as it is for those in caring professions, please let people *care for you* at this moment without your having to reciprocate or "top" their gifts — having the last word, as it were. Let this be the time when the laity experience themselves as the strong and giving ones. Please consult the bishop on any changes or adaptations you contemplate making in the induction, especially any truly unusual gifts or symbols of office. Stuffed animals, entrenching tools (both of which I have seen), or any other things remotely cute, are very seldom appropriate. If something is reasonably anticipated to evoke a giggle, or cause people to dwell on some endearing aspect of your personality, it is very probably better to drop it or save it for the reception. There is, sad to say, in my observation of the use of this service since 1976, a high correlation between the presentation of seriously eccentric symbols and short rectorships. Again, let the congregation take care of you; you will have the next twenty years to express yourself to them.

Let the bishop know whether your family is to be presented with you, and if they are, the names of those family members who will be with you. Please also let the bishop know how you wish to be referred to in the third person. (John, Mother Smith, Mr. Smith, Mrs. Smith, Dean Dana, Canon Candy, etc. *Academic or civil titles are never appropriate in this setting.*)

At the Eucharist

The bishop will ordinarily designate the offerings to your discretionary fund. If you prefer some other designation, that is fine. Either way, the designation should be listed in the service folder.

Please have, if possible, deacons or a deacon to set the table, assist with the book, and elevate the chalice at the great doxology at the end of the eucharistic prayer. Usually the bishop's deacon will perform the last function.

You may choose the eucharistic prayer.

You will join the bishop at the altar, as will the archdeacon. Please invite other "concelebrants" as you may desire and the space permits. Concelebration as practiced in our diocese is described in the ordination customary and the customary for eucharists at which the bishop presides.

The concelebrants will communicate themselves.

Please plan to distribute bread along with the bishop and to assign the chalices as you see fit. If for some reason there are not to be sufficient clergy to administer Holy Communion, the prayer book provides for lay assistants.

Please note the proper post-communion collect; it is best to print it in the service folder so that your Christian name (only), in the form you wish it used, will appear in the place designated.

Ordinarily, you give the blessing.

The dismissal is to be said facing the people, whenever it occurs.

An Alternative

The canons do not require the prayer book institution service, and if you are uncomfortable with its liturgical shape, there is another way. A eucharist, presided at by the bishop or the bishop's representative, may be celebrated. After the prayers of the people, the letter of institution is read. A warden or representative of the parish may read a statement of welcome. The new rector may respond with a few words, the prayer given in the present service, or both. The new rector begins the peace, and the liturgy follows in the usual way, perhaps with the new rector presiding, observing the special practices associated with a liturgy celebrated in the bishop's presence. High revel may follow in the parish house, and gifts of intrinsic and symbolic worth may be given and more speeches by civic and church leaders can be made. Other approaches are of course possible, and you are invited to share your thoughts with the bishop.

Available online at *www.churchpublishing.org/thebishopiscoming*

III. Cluing Them In: "The Postulant's Guide"

Increasingly our clergy are being formed outside the environment of this church's seminaries. The bishop is thus confronted with the problem of the *tradition of the lore*, the passing on of the unwritten traditions and practices that every profession possesses. The specimen given below is an abbreviated version of what I normally distribute, the full text of which includes an element of play not readily understood outside the personal relationship between bishop and postulants. It intentionally focuses on the topics that fascinate seminarians, at least as observed in my time of seminary teaching. Accordingly, rather a lot of ink is given to apparel and terms of address, but the real theme is collegiality.

The Postulant's OTHER Guide
in the Diocese of Bethlehem

Congratulations on your postulancy. In addition to the official diocesan ordination guide prepared by the bishop and Commission on Ministry, I am sending you what follows, hence the title, the *other* guide. This booklet comes from two experiences. The first is that of being asked many questions repeatedly. The second is that of seeing awkward moments occur where people were behaving with the best possible will but just did not have the appropriate information.

Thus this information is for you as you begin your journey, but it is not intended for reaching judgments about people who may have been formed in other ways in other places and at other times. It is an attempt to describe one state of the art; one universe among many possible universes. Like all maps it is a lie if taken too seriously. Thus it is not shared with the aim of disparaging those from other cultures or with other sensibilities. That is, I am trying to be somewhat playfully *descriptive* of some cultural norms in a specific place and time ("northeast corridor" Episcopalians in the early Twenty-First Century). It is well to remember that the only thing worse than a gaffe on one's own part is publicly pointing out someone else's gaffe. This explains the simultaneous unpopularity and fear of fashion critics and gossip columnists.

The Daily Office

Ordained ministry is spiritually demanding and this diocese requires its clergy to have a spiritual director, make retreats, and attend clergy Bible studies and clergy days, all in the service of maintaining and increasing the spiritual and mental health of the clergy. Additionally, clergy need to pray if they are to survive. Consequently as of this moment, and in your own interests, you are expected to say at least Morning and Evening Prayer every day for the rest of your life, alone or with others. Noonday Prayer and Compline are optional, but recommended. The office can be read or sung online, if that helps. It works for the bishop. Point your browser to *http://www.missionstclare.com/*. You may choose English or Spanish. Make it your homepage, perhaps.

Ember Letters

Are herewith abolished. You are expected, per the canon, to visit with the bishop in each of the ember months. It is up to you to make the appointment.

Collars

There is no provision for a "seminarian's collar" in this diocese. A word about clerical dress may be appropriate in this place. The point of any professional costume is to indicate function and availability. When the time does come to don the cloth, please note that in preferred use clergy shirts, vests, and rabats for deacons and priests are black. In the originating period of what we would recognize as western clergy street dress (actually rather recent) it was the black, and not the collar (which came later) that was the indication that one was a member of the clergy or judiciary. I confess to thinking that the introduction of purple shirts in this country in the 1960s and 1970s was a mistake and do not often wear them. A frock coat would work with my figure but I do not have the nerve.

Threads and Accessories

You can find historical "precedent" for anything your heart desires, but this is not really the point of vesture or professional street dress. The most important principle is rather simple, however. *Try to look like you fit in* with the others. You are part, or are preparing to be part, of a collegial ministry: fashion competition and strong personal statements are inappropriate because they are corrosive of collegiality and suggest that you think you are a cut above your colleagues. Simple is best in cassock, alb, surplice, and other things we wear in common. Acting out your issues through what you wear or refuse to wear embarrasses you, your profession, and the church. Apparently my concerns here are not a modern issue: the council held in London in 1268 decreed against clerical costume that was "ridiculous or remarkable."

Acquire a cassock that reaches the top of your shoes, and a surplice nearly that long, for the morning and evening office and for occasions when you are assisting liturgically and an alb is not appropriate. Cassocks do not have little detachable capes (mozettas) unless you are a rector or canon, and they do not have piping of either red or purple unless you are at least a canon. "Cottas" and short surplices of the kind worn in the Roman Church were developed long after the Reformation, and in our setting can claim no place. Anglican-style cassocks require a cincture. Canons and the archdeacon wear a purple cassock for the office and may wear a mass cassock (black with red piping) at the eucharist. In this diocese we use red-purple for canons' choir cassocks.

Acquire a simple white unadorned alb (and amice) or cassock alb, and a simple white rope cincture (some modern albs do not require a cincture[1]). The word "alb" is the abbreviation

---

1. Cinctures (originally belts) seem to have entered in the ninth century as a deliberate attempt to emulate the practice of ancient Israel, and are increasingly seen as dispensable in our own day. Amices, the last of the traditional vestments to be added, were adopted to protect vestments from soil; the combination of modern bathing and laundering practices should make them unnecessary.

for "tunica longa alba" (long white dress). The word alb means "white." Thus, brown, grey, and oatmeal are not appropriate colors, as patristic material emphasizes the whiteness of the vestment. It is the basic and most ancient liturgical garment of bishops, priests, deacons, and other liturgical ministers. Like the cassock, the alb should reach the top of your shoes. If you cannot resist a lace alb, you must wear a cassock underneath it.

As you age, your figure will almost certainly change, and you may need to have a new cassock and alb made. Nothing looks worse than a vestment that has begun to ride mid-calf because of our sagging tissue: all of its lines are distorted. When this day comes, the cincture is still worn over the navel, not snuggled under the paunch or perched above it. As we age further, we inevitably lose height, and further adjustments will be necessary.

Stoles worn over a cassock-alb with no chasuble over them are not crossed, nor are they tied down. They drape over the shoulders freely.

There are, unfortunately, not yet maternity vestments, and one trusts that the women clergy of the diocese have worked this out and perhaps have a trove from which to lend each other vesture of appropriate dimensions for use during pregnancy. Fuller chasubles and albs, and longer stoles might well be shared.

Wear black shoes, freshly shined, when officiating in liturgy. Shiny buckles are to be avoided. Fashions in women's shoes are somewhat flexible, but it is to be remembered that classically, gentlemen do not wear loafers with suits. If you decide to wear loafers, tassels and pennies are to be avoided with vestments. Except on military duty, at disaster sites, or on very informal occasions, in our region of the country cowboy boots, boat shoes, sandals (except in the habit of religious orders), and work boots have a somewhat affected look in the liturgical ensemble. Very seriously, how we dress shows respect for other people and for the circumstances in which worship occurs. It is not an ideal world and people are "only human:" if you appear at the most sacred moment of most people's week looking like you are stuck on yourself or have just been to a rodeo or a beach movie, do not wonder if they do not take seriously what you do or say in the liturgy. It should not be that way, perhaps, but nonetheless it is.

I accept that the majority of clergy are "intuitive-feeling" types in the sense that psychological testing uses the expression, but the truth remains that in how you appear in the liturgical assembly *you do not gotta be you.* When all is said and done, if it's about you, your taste, or your issues with authority, it's probably not helpful to God's people and should not be worn. If thinking this way raises very strong feelings for you, we should talk sooner rather than later.

You will notice that for Sunday visitations, the bishop's vestments are rather modest. Most of our churches are of a size where the vestments appropriate to the cathedral or larger churches would overpower the liturgy and not contribute to worship. I mention this so that you will consider that ideally chasubles and copes should be designed for a particular room. While there is nothing wrong with clergy owning or even collecting vestments, only those should be worn in public that work in the particular space. If one will err, it should be on the side of simplicity. In general, before you start building any collection of vesture, please remember that vestments are distinguished more by the quality, shape and cut of their fabric, than by the amount of adornment they carry. Avoid anything with actual words on it.

As a postulant, candidate, deacon, or priest, you are not to wear a cross as part of your liturgical vesture (I prescind entirely, but reluctantly, from the question of so decorating acolytes and choirs). With street clothes you may wear a cross on a cord if you are connected with a religious order where this is required and a special cross is issued; other than that, crosses are not used by deacons and priests with a collar. In the liturgical vesture of the catholic west, unlike the orthodox east, crosses are part of the insignia of bishops, not an accessory for all clerics. (There is no Anglican rule of silver crosses for priests and gold for bishops — many bishops and even archbishops wear silver.) You are free to wear whatever you want under your vestments and shirt, of course. Notwithstanding all of this, if you feel compelled to wear a cross with your clergy shirt, put it in your breast pocket and avoid the chain. Some women wear rather small crosses that are clearly jewelry and not an imitation of pectoral crosses, and that is acceptable. I do understand that Lutherans, who cling to the idea that there is but one order of ministry, and many protestants, wear large, even enormous, pectoral crosses with vesture. We do not share their ecclesiology and this distinction will have visual results.

Similarly, try not to wear rings other than rings given in troth when serving at the liturgy, because in worship a ring is a liturgical significator. Additionally, jewelry that can be seen from more than a few feet away should not be worn when ministering liturgically. This includes watches and anything that dangles from perforations in your flesh. Military decorations are not worn on the tippet under any circumstances in this country. Tippets are best not equipped with seals, which in our country are saved for blazers.

It hardly needs to be said that the use of the biretta in the eucharistic liturgy is not an Anglican practice, and has been suppressed in the Roman Church since Vatican II and central heating, perhaps not in that order. Head cover of some kind (Canterbury caps are a little more Anglican) along with the cloak make very good sense when one is ministering out of doors at say, funerals or Rogation processions. In some parts of the Anglican Communion, head covering is *carried* during choir offices, but this seems rather a lot of work. The cloak (*cappa nigra*) is not a vestment, and for warmth's sake may be placed over whatever you have on liturgically.

Mega-Don't: there are never any situations in which it is proper to cross your legs while wearing vestments. In traditional vestments such posture looks uncouth and dissonant; in the cassock-alb it looks slovenly or even indecent.

You will in all probability soon be assisting at the altar if you are not already doing so. This is your first chance to experience collegiality and coordination. The practices and acts that are to be followed are those of the presider/celebrant. For instance, if the presider makes the sign of the cross during "unite us to your Son in his sacrifice," in Prayer B, so do you. If not, it is not well for you to do so. Upstaging the rector has a corrosive effect on people's perceived but unarticulated ecclesiology, and sometimes has career implications for you. If a practice in the parish where you are assisting actually offends your conscience, as opposed to your sensibilities, it is essential that you thoroughly discuss it with the rector.

How to Write a Letter

Even though church letters are very often business letters, the ecclesiastical custom, especially when writing to clergy with whom you are not at the moment entirely enraged, is to end the salutation with the more friendly comma rather than the colon usual in secular correspondence. You will also see "The Reverend" abbreviated as "The Rev'd," an English practice; because the final consonant is used in that form, a period does not follow the abbreviation.

To your own bishop:
The Rt. Rev. Jane D. Smith
333 Wyandotte, etc.
Dear Bishop,

or,
Dear Bishop Jane,

chilly or archaic,
My dear Bishop,

To the Presiding Bishop
The Most Reverend Jane Smith
815 Second Avenue, etc.
Dear Bishop Smith,

To somebody else's bishop:
The Rt. Rev. John D. Smith
etc.
Dear Bishop Smith,

To an archdeacon	*To a canon*
The Ven. Jane Doe	The Rev. Canon John Smith
Etc.	etc.
Dear Archdeacon Doe,	Dear Canon Smith,

To a dean
The Very Rev. John Doe
Etc.
Dear Dean Doe,

By long tradition (going back to before there were surnames), bishops often sign only their first name, or in more formal correspondence, may use their see as a surname ("William, Pennsylvania"), although this latter practice has a ducal ring and is usually saved for moments when heavy artillery is called for. Do not mistake a one-word signature for an invitation to address bishops by their first names in conversation. They will tell you that directly if it is the case. Remember, the use of titles creates a safe, respectful, and professional space, and thus it is for the sake of the safe relationship that you will probably not be invited to use the bishop's Christian name alone. It is not about you; it is about space for work.

Which leads us to

Titles

Once ordained, you are, in the third person, The Reverend Your Full Name. "The Reverend Father/Mother" before your name is not Anglican usage, nor is "Reverend" by itself a term of reference or address usual in the Episcopal Church. Sometimes "Mr." or "Ms." is substituted for the first name upon a second reference ("The Rev. Mr. Smith will also preach...") but this is almost entirely disused in our region. Mr., Mrs., and Ms. are fine by themselves, although a bit archaic in much of the country.

Speaking descriptively, in this diocese the general practice is that clergy are addressed informally as "Father" or "Mother" with first or last name. Again, the use of titles creates a safe

professional space in which ministry can happen without imply-
ing or demanding *artificial intimacy;* in the end it protects the
faithful more than it shows respect for your role, although it does
do both. Some women clergy locally use other forms of address,
given the variety of thinking about maternal titles, and this matter is still in flux. He will do his best, but please do not take it
as a slight if the bishop does not remember particular forms of
address you may have developed.

A cross, usually looking like a plus-sign, is a customary but
not mandatory or universal part of the signature of bishops; in
the last century a plus after the name became the fashion among
some presbyters, although reasons for this are hard to explain.
Notwithstanding any of that, using a plus sign as a form of address or term of reference is always incorrect (never say "Dear
Jane+," or "according to +Helen," except in jests of exquisite
dryness). The use of plusses by priests certainly would be appropriate only as a signature, never as a term of address or a reference
in the third person, except, again, in jest.

If you use a plus, it is with the signature only and means that
you don't use any other designator.

Correct: Jane+ or Jane Smith+.

Incorrect: The Rev. Jane Smith+, Fr. John Smith+, or using the
plus sign as part of a typed signature block under your written
signature.

Rural deans do not style themselves "The Very Reverend," a
title reserved to deans of institutions such as cathedrals and seminaries where there is an on-site staff. The term Dean comes from
the Latin, indicating someone who presided over a staff of (at
least) ten.

If you desire to indicate academic status on your letterhead,
the degrees go after your name in ascending order of importance/
rarity. Thus earned degrees go first, honorary degrees second,
and higher honors last: "The Reverend Your Name, M.Div., J.D.,
D.D., F.R.H.S., M.B.E." Only the highest degree in each category
is used (thus, not both M.Div. and D. Min). If you have two Ph.D.
and three D.D. degrees, you are still only Ph.D., D.D.

The practice of addressing people as "Doctor" varies from culture to culture. In America the old rules of our New World culture still apply: only with medicos and clergy do Americans use doctoral titles as a form of address in normal social intercourse. In first-tier educational institutions in America, faculty are never addressed as Doctor, as a doctorate is merely a credential everybody has. Practices vary on the lower tiers where possession of scholarly credentials may be more remarkable.

"The Reverend Doctor" sounds very grand, doesn't it? It is best not to use it when referring to self, ever. In any event, "The Rev. Dr." is, very strictly speaking, only to be used about those who have an honorary degree in the theological sphere, the D.D. or its relatives. This doctoral status was originally granted only to those who had made some important contribution to the life of the church and thus became its doctor (in the original sense of teacher). "The Reverend Doctor" has now been stretched to include those who have earned a doctorate in a theological subject, but again, this can seem a little pretentious when used about oneself. It is completely incorrect for someone who has a doctoral degree in a non-theological subject to refer to self in church circles as "The Reverend Doctor" — it is claiming a credential and authority in the church that one simply does not have. It would make as much sense as walking into a hospital and expecting to be called "Doctor" by the nursing staff because you once wrote a thesis on Proust.

The time to be generous with honorifics is when writing to or about others. If your friend or colleague has earned an academic theological degree or a D.Min, or has been honored with a D.D., it is very thoughtful and courteous to write to that friend or colleague as "The Reverend Doctor J. Doe." They, of course, will be too modest to reply in that style, limiting their degree to initials after their name on the letterhead, but they will very much appreciate your noticing.

If using a degree is desired, in America your signature line in a letter is "(The Rev.) J. Doe, Ph.D." and not "The Rev. Dr. J. Doe."

If "Dr." is used, the degree may not follow the name ("Dr. J. Doe, M.D.," would be incorrect).

Please do not ever list the bishop as "The Rt. Rev. Dr." in service folders. It's just too much. Furthermore, it is useful to note that by decree of a very early General Convention, our bishops are forbidden to use titles like "Your Grace," "My Lord," "Your Excellency," etc. You are accordingly asked to address the bishop simply as "Bishop." There is a great deal to be said for this in America, where the episcopate confers no earthly lordship. And please do not kiss the ring.

Select Bibliography

Bishops, particularly new bishops, do not have a great deal of reading time, so these two lists are intentionally quite short.

Theory

Chauvet, Louis-Marie. *The Sacraments: The Word of God at the Mercy of the Body*. Collegeville, MN: Liturgical Press, 2001. [Although some theological translation is needed for Anglican readers, this is in some ways the freshest treatment of the sacraments available and satisfies the philosopher as well as the theologian.]

House of Bishops, ECUSA. *The Ministry of Bishops*. New York: Trinity Institute, 1991. [The last testament of the generation of bishops who brought us the 1979 prayer book. Although its answers are minimalist and focus a great deal on function, it still asks all the right questions.]

Kavanagh, Aidan Joseph. *Confirmation: Origins and Reform*. New York: Pueblo, 1988.

Kavanagh, Aidan Joseph. *The Shape of Baptism*. Collegeville, MN: Liturgical Press, 1991, repr. [Both of Kavanagh's concise books should be read before painting oneself into a corner on questions of initiation.]

Mitchell, Leonel L. *Praying Shapes Believing*. Harrisburg, PA: Morehouse, 1991. [Simply the best explanation of the 1979 liturgy.]

Wright, John Robert, ed. *On Being a Bishop: Papers from the Moscow Consultation 1992*. New York: Church Hymnal Corporation, 1992. [International, ecumenical symposium on *episkope*.]

Practice

Buchanan, Colin, ed. *The Bishop in Liturgy.* Bramcotte: Grove Books, 1984. [Evangelical alternative to this guide.]

Galley, Howard E. *The Ceremonies of the Eucharist: A Guide to Celebration.* Cambridge, MA: Cowley Publications, 1989. [Fairly strictly Roman alternative to this guide in its treatment of episcopal ceremonial.]

Gasslein, Bernadette. *Preparing and Evaluating Liturgy.* Collegeville, MN: Liturgical Press, 1997.

Mitchell, Leonel L. *Pastoral and Occasional Liturgies.* Cambridge, MA: Cowley Publications, 1998. [A work primarily for parish clergy, but also contains a mainstream, "Associated Parishes" approach to episcopal ceremonial.]

International Commission on English in the Liturgy. *Ceremonial of Bishops.* Collegeville, MN: Liturgical Press, 1989. [Current Roman use.]

www.ingramcontent.com/pod-product-compliance
Lightning Source LLC
Jackson TN
JSHW080852211224
75817JS00002B/17

* 9 7 8 0 8 9 8 6 9 5 4 2 7 *